MAKING SENSE OUT OF LIFE

Westminster Press Books by
CHARLES DUELL KEAN

Making Sense Out of Life
The Inward Cross

Making Sense
OUT OF
Life

CHARLES DUELL KEAN

Philadelphia

THE WESTMINSTER PRESS

COPYRIGHT, MCMLIV, BY W. L. JENKINS

Library of Congress Catalog Card No.: 54–9446

PRINTED IN THE UNITED STATES OF AMERICA

Contents

Foreword

This book is the result of fifteen years of pastoral experience in which my first objective has been to help adult men and women to make sense out of their lives in spite of the fact that daily living seemed so often meaningless. In many instances these people had been exposed to the Christian tradition, but very rarely did they see any connection between the religious symbols passed on to them and the problems with which they were confronted.

My pastoral task, therefore, has been to make the treasures of Christian faith available in such a way that modern men and women could find them to be what they were always intended to be — the only way of making sense out of life without falsifying issues or ignoring significant parts of the problem. My firm conviction is that the Christian faith is just as functional in the twentieth century as in the first, but that the task of interpretation and application is never completed.

My first thanks in connection with this book must go to the several hundred men and women who, both in group classes and in individual conferences, have helped me to work through these understandings. They have taught me much more than I have ever taught them. Most of them were my parishioners at Grace Church, Kirkwood, Missouri, but others have been members of summer conferences in Maryland, Virginia, and North Carolina.

My hope is that this book may turn out to be a useful tool for laymen facing the same task by themselves and for clergymen whose job is the same as mine. My job still goes on, as I try to make these understandings available to other men and women in a new community, and I hope to use this book as a resource for them.

I should like to express my particular appreciation to Rev. Edward P. Dentzer, for four years my partner at Grace Church, Kirkwood, and to Mrs. Clarence H. Dawson, parish secretary there. Mrs. Dawson worked over the manuscript during innumerable revisions and has given many valuable suggestions about making the content clearer. Finally, may I express my appreciation to Dr. Paul L. Meacham, of The Westminster Press, for encouragement and advice leading up to the final publication of the book.

CHARLES DUELL KEAN.

The Church of the Epiphany,
Washington, D.C.

CHAPTER I

Christianity Makes Sense Out of Life

CHRISTIANITY makes sense out of life.

Without the Christian faith to provide the perspective in which we can see our experience deeply as well as broadly, life is nonsense. Things do not add up to an intelligible whole. There are surds on the one hand and a continuing note of chaos on the other.

During the darkest days of World War II, the late William Temple, Archbishop of Canterbury, wrote in a *Christian News-Letter* supplement, "We must still claim that Christianity enables us to 'make sense' of the world, not meaning that we can show that it is sense, but with the more literal and radical meaning of making into sense what, till it is transformed, is largely nonsense — a disordered chaos waiting to be reduced to order as the Spirit of God gives it shape."

The Christian faith, in this radical sense of providing a totally different point of view from anything the world can produce from its own historical, political, economic, and social processes, provides that note of clarity without which there is no way of dealing creatively with the chaos of our modern world. While man can do many things about the results of this primary disorder in the very scheme of things, unless something enables him to cut his way through to the basic human problem, he will always be providing patchwork solutions which never prove to be adequate.

What Paul wrote to the first century Christian Church of Corinth is still true: " For God, who commanded the light to shine out of darkness, hath shined in our hearts, to give us the light of the knowledge of the glory of God in the face of Jesus Christ." Whatever set of symbols we may use — light shining in darkness, clarity overcoming chaos, peace prevailing over conflict, life winning the victory over death — the same principle is involved. For Christians, God has provided through Jesus Christ a creative way of dealing with the real problem of life.

The next verse in the passage from the Second Epistle to the Corinthians bears out the point we are trying to make: " But we have this treasure in earthen vessels, that the excellency of the power may be of God, and not of us." Christianity can be related, it is true, to the evolutionary development of man's religiousness. Christian understandings may be paraphrased in philosophical and scientific terms which illustrate the depth of insight attainable by the human mind. But that which enables us to make sense out of life is something unique, something discontinuous with the normal processes of human history. For Christians who take it seriously this is the gift of God.

The way God has provided for us is essentially a matter of relationships — with him and with one another through him. The picture is that of triangle — God, me, my brother; me, God, my brother; me, my brother, God; God, my brother, me; my brother, me, God; my brother, God, me. Whichever way we go around the triangle, regardless of the position from which we start, the meaning is the same. This triangular relationship is made possible by the sustaining power of the Holy Spirit in the life of the Christian fellowship, which empowers people to meet life from within the relationship in a way which man outside it cannot either grasp or appreciate.

We approach the same detailed problems that anyone else approaches from a different background. The problems of everyday life in every area, from our homes to the international scene, still remain as important as ever. They are just as urgent for the man who is consciously Christian as they are for the secular sociologist, the political scientist, or the economist. In a very fundamental sense they are even more urgent, because they have a bearing upon our eternal destiny as well as upon our immediate fortunes. But, as Christians, we meet the difficulties of the world in a new spirit, for we are members of a fellowship which finds its center in the love of God and dares to live as if this were the most important reality in the universe.

To make such a claim about Christian faith sounds either bold or naïve in a day when men are becoming increasingly aware of the complexities of life. A change in the administration of the American Government has highlighted for everybody the fact that many of the issues, which seem so simple in campaign oratory, are actually so ramified in their causes and connections that it is very hard to make serious changes in policy. The present international tension is rooted in at least a half century of history, and all the tentative moves in this or that direction, to restore stability to the world's political and economic life, are related to the difficulties now before us. It is not simply a matter of the individuals or even the party in control in Washington, or London, or Moscow.

To take another example from the world of government, we are told that it is next to impossible for any congressman to digest the vast amount of data, in the form of reports, surveys, and analyses, which has a bearing on vital bills upon which he must vote. Yet the only way to maintain or change governmental policy is through the votes of congressmen, who are supposedly in a position to see farther than the man in the street. When the underlying facts of administering a large industrial nation are considered, even major tinkering with the machinery of government does not seem to offer much promise of making the job of congressmen clear and simple. Even with all its obvious merits, the report of the Hoover Commission cannot promise a United States where problems of national policy can be considered in the way local questions of bridges and ditches could be discussed in an early nineteenth century New England town meeting.

In the more intimate areas of the family and individual personality, the depth psychologists and the educators are showing us that problems are equally complex if they involve experience over a period of years, the influence of cultural factors, and the kind of pressures one is subject to at the moment. Decision-making is not easy once the total situation is viewed, and the only people who seem to find it relatively easy to make choices are those who do so apparently " off the top of their heads," without too much thought for background or consequences.

The claim made for the Christian faith is not an escape from, nor an evasion of, the complexities of modern life. These problems are here with us as part of the agenda with which we must deal, because we live in this particular moment of history. But the Christian affirmation is that it will make a tremendous difference in the way one is able to deal with the issues of the day if the underlying problem of man has been met and is being faced. Christianity claims to provide the only complete way of living through this underlying problem; and Christianity dares to believe that this will have a most profound effect upon the way people deal with the problems of family, business, community, national, and international affairs.

Anybody who has ever watched little children begin kindergarten will notice that some children will withdraw from any but minimum participation in what the class is doing. Other children will be confused and show their bewilderment by erratic behavior — laughter and tears not quite in keeping with what is going on. Some children will act aggressively through talking or pushing other children around. But there will be some who will be able to accept the situation and begin learning from the out-set, who will be sufficiently secure so that they are not afraid of "losing their inmost souls" as they try to do things and some-times fail, and as they try to get along with teacher and class-mates and sometimes fail at this too. These children may not be brighter intellectually than the others. They may not be more talented. They may often have serious handicaps in behavior as well as in physical equipment. The decisive difference is that their family background is sufficiently dynamic in its pattern of mutual acceptance to allow the little kindergartners to face the complexities of classroom life and do the best they can with what they have there.

The reference to the kindergarten situation is just an analogy. It would be a mistake to see more in it than that. But in some parallel way Christianity provides its adherents with an accept-ing point of view toward life, growing out of a dynamic pattern of relationships with God and with other people, so that they can face the problems of the world without the fear of completely losing their own souls as they try to deal with what is before them. Technical problems remain just as technical, but our re-lationship to them is different, because our relationship to God and to one another is different.

We have been saying that the root problem of the modern world is religious, and that Christianity provides the only thor-oughgoing religious answer. The chaos is not simply the result of a wide variety of crosscurrents in the world of economic, political, and social action. It is the result, if it is really chaos, of the people who have to deal with economic, political, and social problems being lost people, with no "spiritual home" upon which they may count. Christianity provides those who have really "put on Christ," to use Paul's words, with such a home, and with the assurance that comes from being able to depend on this eternal reality, even when the problems of the world are overwhelming.

Such a view of Christianity is, perhaps, a little different from what the modern world has come to understand, since we think of the Christian faith primarily as dynamic relationships — not a static set of opinions. We think of the Christian faith as a bond of union between God and man and, therefore, between man and his fellow man, which does not simply stand like a rock against which waves dash but, rather, is in itself a truly creative force. Christian faith, so understood, can have a positive influence upon the life of men and nations and upon the whole course of history in which they are involved.

The Early Christian Church may not have used terms such as these, but this was its understanding. Paul did not go out into the Mediterranean world to get people to exchange one set of theoretical opinions for another. He went out to share a creative " way of life "; and the phrase " way of life " meant something much more vital than a mutual agreement about ethical norms. It meant that people were brought into a new family, a living relationship, a history-changing movement, where the strength of the whole was really greater than the sum of the parts, and all could know it at first hand for themselves.

The traditional word symbols of Christianity — incarnation, cross, atonement, resurrection, Pentecost, Body of Christ, etc. — were originally ways of describing this relationship in functional terms so that its application to life would be clearer. These word symbols, as used this way, are tremendously charged. The adjective " mere " cannot be applied to them at all. But symbols they are, because they are terms that describe dynamically how men are related to God and to each other under the influence of Christ.

Through the use of these symbols the Christian faith offers clarity to mankind to overcome the world's confusion. But the world does not see it — partly because many people are unaware of the real function of Christian word symbols, and then because many people are afraid of the relationship being described, once they catch a hint of what is really implied. In other words, the world is non-Christian both because it does not understand the issue and because it does not want to face its own underlying problems. An intellectual clarification of the issue will not suffice because it will leave untouched the real anxiety that tears our hearts and disturbs our social relations.

The first part of the problem, then, is to help people to appreciate the clarity that Christian faith provides. This involves helping them to recognize that the Christian "language" is actually talking about problems that concern them. People cannot understand answers that apparently do not apply to their actual questions. One of the greatest obstacles to the cause of Christianity in the modern world is that it speaks an idiom that few people use with any sureness. It is not so much a matter of vocabulary as it is of appreciating the relevance of the symbols to the actual problems men and women are facing in everyday life. They do not see the connection between these traditional terms and doctrines and the real problems of personality, family, business, community, and national and international affairs which confront them.

The other, and perhaps even more serious, side of the problem is that the world for generations has pleaded ignorance of the meaning of the word symbols or has leveled charges of irrelevance at them as a means of avoiding facing the deeper issues of life. While everybody wants to make sense out of his own experience, he wants to do it his own way. He does not want to face, at least at the outset, his own share of responsibility for the confusion that besets him and the world. We do not like to deal profoundly with the problem of our egotism, even though we all agree that this would be a nicer, happier world if everybody were more generous and accepting. When the issue is raised, our first impulse is to dodge it on one pretext or another. Along with the problem of the relevance of the word symbols of Christian tradition to the actual situations in which we are involved is the associated problem of recognizing that each of these terms is a challenge — a finger pointed directly at our hearts. To respond to the challenge is to be forced to look at ourselves in a way most of us would rather avoid.

This modern world still has a fair intellectual acquaintance with the Christian gospel. The familiar words are heard, at least in churches, and sometimes are used as literary allusions. The institutions of the Christian religion continue to function, often with real appeal and wide response. Yet the fact remains that even those most closely identified with Christian institutions and most familiar with Christian terminology do not seem to be able to make its symbols very effective in the world around them. It is not that the modern world consciously rejects the Christian challenge. On the one hand, it is largely unaware of the Christian issue, and on the other hand it can use its "ignorance" as a way of avoiding the challenge to its own presuppositions.

In this so-called Christian civilization, men and women do not interpret life's meaning for themselves by the Christian tradition. Few people seem to realize very deeply that the symbols of the Christian faith comprise a language which enables its users to interpret life's meaning more profoundly and accurately than does any other tongue. It is not because men are uninterested in interpreting life's meaning, however, that they are unaware of the functions of the Christian faith. It is, rather, that they are not aware that Christianity is supposed to be a relevant answer to the fundamental questions that everyone is really asking in his own heart and through his social actions.

Anyone who has ever had to answer a child's question knows that one of the great difficulties in replying is that of translating the answer into terms that the child can understand without emasculating the issue in the process. Language and maturity go hand in hand. Without an adequate language, people cannot analyze problems and relate themselves creatively to them. The fact that beginners in any learned profession — medicine, law, social service, theology, and others — tend to acquire a jargon at the outset of their studies is an indication that they are trying to relate themselves understandingly and creatively to real issues, which cannot be appreciated easily in the ordinary language of the drawing room. It is a sign of maturity to be able to dispense with professional jargon without oversimplifying issues. Yet it is true that without adequate word symbols people cannot communicate with one another about anything except trivialities, nor can they articulate their own problems so profoundly as they need to articulate them. Professional languages serve a very real purpose, not only as intellectual short cuts in communication, but even more as a means of relating the speaker to significant questions and answers.

A superficial familiarity with either a foreign language or a professional vocabulary may easily obscure one's awareness that these word symbols are more than labels, or that they describe living relationships. A superficial acquaintance with the Christian tradition may familiarize people with the better-known terms and their more common definitions without in any way raising in their minds the question as to whether these terms are not perhaps descriptions of the problems they are trying to face.

The following chapters are an attempt to present the Christian faith as a language by means of which men and women may understand themselves, their relationships to other people, and their direction for living more profoundly and more accurately than they can through any other means. The attempt will be made to relate Christianity to the questions that men and women are asking just because they are alive, and to show how a functional interpretation of the Christian tradition makes possible a creative faith on the part of free men and women.

In order to make such an interpretation possible, it is necessary to explore the meaning of religion as a category of life for the purpose of discovering why men and women are interested in religions. Such an exploration, however, requires the elimination of preconceptions, which define the category of religion by existing religious systems and institutions, rather than seeing these as expressions of a basic tendency in human nature. The thesis of this book is that all men, because of the construction of human nature, must wrestle somehow with the problem of meaningfulness, and that this is the basis of all religious thought and action.

Christianity will not be presented as one religion among many, however, but as that faith which enables men to deal truly and creatively with their fundamental problems without distorting reality. Whether other religious interpretations could do the same thing is not a significant issue here. The conviction is that men and women take Christianity seriously, not because of speculative inquiry, but because they find it the living means of that kind of relationship to life's fundamental demand which enables them to make sense out of their experience in a real world.

In a fundamental sense, Christianity will always be a foreign language to those who are not identified by vital conviction with the Christian fellowship. It cannot be acquired from the environment — only familiarity with its words as words can be picked up this way. It cannot be acquired merely by identification with any religious institution or organization, no matter how ancient its history or how large its membership. Christianity is necessarily a foreign language to those who are satisfied with the kind of questions they are asking about life's meaning and the kind of answers they are accepting, from whatever source they take them.

Although the Christian faith can never be the native tongue for anyone, it can become the language of his " adopted country " in the double sense involved in naturalization — acceptance by the country and identification by the person. Once a man's appreciation of his own predicament and his awareness of the significance of the Christian symbols meet, "naturalization" in this sense is a real possibility. Then the Christian language becomes more real to him than the tongue he speaks in ordinary conversation, because it enables him to know his own heart before the real God.

This is the real secret of clarity in the world's confusion. To shift the analogy again from that of language and country to that of family and home will bring out the same basic point in another way. Every family has ways of speaking and acting that carry greater significance for the members than the acts or words in themselves. The outsider can only guess what is meant; he cannot share in the sense of power and assurance that is imparted. Whether it is a caress, a nickname, or a fleeting expression within the family, it can convey the message, "I believe in you, win, lose, or draw."

Within the family, however, this language of the heart is not just a way of communicating. It is in itself a dynamic force. It strengthens the members as they face their problems in a changing world, and as they grow older, and as they encounter new situations. The power of the family is not simply the result of its being there. Rather it serves as the living setting for the struggle of existence. It adapts itself to the needs of its members in particular situations. It never solves their problems for them, because that is not its function, but it stands behind them as they wrestle with circumstance on the basis of their faith.

It is in this way that the Christian religion provides clarity in the world's chaos, and this is in sharp contradiction to man's ordinary experience. The normal alternative to chaos is order. In his desire for order man sets up systems of control — in the family, in the business world, and in national and international life. But order, sought as an end in itself, becomes regimentation, dictatorship, suppression of the spirit, and the death of freedom. Our modern world finds itself facing a tragic dilemma — on the one hand, chaos and freedom, in the sense of free opportunity to create and contribute; and on the other hand, order and death in the form of a collectivized life from which the spark is missing. All too often the two alternatives seem to lead each to the opposite. Individual experience and social history, therefore, become a frustrating sequence of creative outbreaks in a chaotic world which lacks solid foundations, and systematic control of affairs in an orderly world without a soul.

The effect of Christianity upon men is to make it possible for them to cut through this dilemma. Within the family, freedom and order sustain, instead of contradicting, each other. In this manner the Christian faith makes possible a clear-eyed facing of problems by men and women whose relationship to God and to mankind is on a firm but dynamic basis. For this reason they can learn from experience. They can adapt their heritage to meet the demands of new situations. They may not know all there is to know about any of the practical problems of life with which they must deal. Nevertheless, they are free to go ahead and do the best they can with what they have where they are, because one thing is sure — they count for something in this universe.

In this kind of dynamic relationship to God and to our fellow men, we can use the great traditional word symbols of Christian experience continually to reaffirm the meaning of our place in the universe, and then to throw light upon the path before us and upon the obstacles in our way. Christianity, so appreciated, is the family spirit of the children of God, daring to meet the real problems of the real world in the freedom in which Christ has made us free, holding the faith in "unity of the Spirit in the bond of peace," and in righteousness of life.

CHAPTER II

The Purpose of Religion

CHRISTIANITY makes sense out of life because it goes to the heart of man's underlying problem — confusion as to the meaning of life itself. Because the issue is really religious, the answer too must be religious.

The purpose of all religion, Christian or not, is to enable people to answer the question, Who am I? in such a way that all the facts are taken into account. An adequate answer to the question must be in terms of life as well as theory, for we are living persons — making decisions, accepting responsibility, responding to demands in a world where situations are continually changing. Likewise, an adequate answer must provide for the whole broad range of our contacts with other people and groups and with social forces and their effect upon us, and also for the depth of our own personalities, which can never be completely explained in terms of external influences.

The Christian faith gives this kind of answer to the underlying religious question, Who am I? so that on the basis of the answer we can find ourselves able to decide and act. We are never completely at home in this world as the Christian faith sees it, and we should not expect to become so. The search for " peace of mind " is very often an evasion. However, we are able to live in the world and find meaning for our choices and a creative kind of relationship with other people.

21

How the Christian faith makes this possible will be explained in later chapters. The important thing to realize at the outset is that this is the real purpose of all religion: to provide an answer to the question, Who am I? Because a great many people do not appreciate this, they tend to reject what they think religion to be while they act "religiously" at the same time without knowing it. People also affirm religious loyalties, but actually handle their problems of life's meaning on the basis of an implicit religion which contradicts the tenets they claim to accept. It is not hard to see many examples of both attitudes and to recognize the confusion which results.

Christianity makes sense out of life in a religious way. This raises the question as to whether Christianity is one religion among many or Religion with a capital " R." The only honest answer is that to Christians it must be both at the same time, and it can only become available to non-Christians when it becomes so. Yet we must admit that Christianity is one of the many ways by which men have sought to find meaning for life. Paul Tillich tells us in *The Courage to Be* that the only real alternative is Stoicism — the courageous bearing up under difficulty. Gerald Heard and others of his point of view have tried to conceive of a " religion " embracing all the various ways used by men. The fact remains that Christianity can be compared functionally with other possible ways of trying to make sense out of life, but it can provide the answer only for those for whom it becomes indeed The Way.

Perhaps the role of the Christian faith — providing clarity in the world's confusion — could be better appreciated if we were clearer as to the purpose of religion in general, not just Christianity but any religion, whether called such or not. When a person is acting religiously, what is he doing? Or, to put it another way, if a man from Mars were to observe the whole range of human behavior in a variety of activities, what would he group together in the category "religion"? The thesis of this volume is that religion primarily refers to making sense out of experience — as in the answer to the question, Who am I? — so that real people have some basis upon which to make decisions in connection with their real problems.

No subject is more widely discussed than religion today, but confusion as to its meaning and purpose is widespread. If this were only a matter of the meaning of an English word, the problem could be handled by coining other terms. But the confusion really suggests that men today are finding serious difficulty in understanding the meaning of their own lives and in interpreting the deeper implications of the problems of their world.

The famous McCollum case, decided by the United States Supreme Court in March, 1948, illustrates the confusion. The point at issue was whether public schools could be used for religious instruction under the sponsorship of organized groups. The editorial comments on both sides of the case equated religion with the official programs of Protestants, Roman Catholics, and Jews. They were implying that opposition to denominational instruction was in itself "antireligious," rather than recognizing it to be the line of a competing naturalistic religion which used different words. The man from Mars would have seen that Mrs. McCollum was trying to do in her way what the sponsors of the denominational classes were in their way — find meaning for life by answering the question, Who am I?

By limiting the use of the term "religion" to the official programs of denominations, the commentators left a whole area of human thought and action without adequate recognition, and illustrated the confusion of our times. However, when religion is considered primarily as the interpretation of experience, the arguments on the McCollum case do not really make sense. To ask whether a person is in favor of or against religion is about as sensible as asking him whether he is in favor of or against digestion or breathing. One may have his theories of diet, or he may regard the study of physiology as a waste of time, but he can hardly dispense with eating.

Another example of the same basic confusion occurred several years ago when Dr. George Gallup, director of the American Institute of Public Opinion, revealed the results of an international survey on the number of people in various countries who said they believed in God. Conclusions were drawn from the array of answers. But the fundamental matter — whether the repliers had the same understanding of the question — was ignored. Can there be any significance at all to opinions about belief in God that do not at the same time indicate a general context shared by all?

Does the question of the existence of God really mean anything on the level of objective opinion? To those who look at religion functionally, the question is not so much whether people do or do not say they believe in God as it is a question of what kind of demands they accept as undeniable, as incontrovertible, in the course of everyday living. The gods whom men obey, whether or not they ever use the three-letter monosyllable "GOD," give some indication of what they are likely to do in living situations, while their theoretical opinions may or may not have any relationship to their real concern.

A completely passive life, responsive to no demands at all, may be said to be godless in this practical sense. People may cherish prejudice against the use of certain words or, again, they may be wedded to certain symbols regardless of their content. The real issue is not one's preference in vocabulary, but the actual premises one accepts in making decisions for himself. The life without premises, if there be such, is the life without any god at all. A Communist, who is ideologically committed against the word "God" as he happens to understand its use in Western culture is, nevertheless, consciously subject to an assumption which governs his life and the choices he makes. Other people may regard the god he worships as false, but to deny that he has a god in the functional sense is to cut religion apart from life and make religion meaningless.

A cretin or a Mongolian idiot, who lives in a world of indiscriminate succession, in which there is no distinction at all between events, may be said to have no religion or to be godless. If a person feels that there is some qualitative distinction between standing for a half hour on a street corner on a cold, sleety, winter night, while waiting alone for a streetcar, and a half hour spent in delightful company listening to great music, that person indicates that he has some kind of faith and that he lives by some kind of demands.

Religion is a manner of dealing with experience rather than an objective set of opinions or customs or rituals. A man's religion is the way he reduces to some kind of order the complex of contradictory and often conflicting relationships and events. Since life is not self-explanatory, in that all the circumstances of our lives and the situations in which we find ourselves are not equally conducive to a simple, clear appreciation of what life is all about, men have to organize their experiences in line with assumptions of some kind. There may be infinite variety as to religions, but wherever men act, consciously or unconsciously, on the basis of convictions as to their own place in the universe, they are, functionally speaking, religious.

To understand a man's religion, therefore, it is more important to appreciate the premises underlying his thinking and his behavior than to consider only the conclusions he has reached or the system he has accepted. As a matter of fact, men may be alike in their premises and, because of differences in educational background, be quite dissimilar in their intellectual expressions. And they may be identical as regards the creeds, codes of conduct, and cult requirements they accept and quite unlike in their basic assumptions. Only the latter are religious in a functional sense.

The result of confusing religion with the conclusions that individuals and groups have reached regarding the detailed practice and expression of their faiths has been to make most so-called religious controversy utterly fruitless. When we debate results alone, we do not really take hold of real questions. We confuse shadow and substance, and while we may easily grow emotional when our institutional practices are under fire, or when we dislike the dogmatic practices of others, we are not really talking to each other at all. Under the circumstances, it is not surprising that most discussions of the subject generate more heat than light.

In spite of the misunderstandings current in modern culture about the meaning of religion and whether there is or is not a God, religion is actually a very vital issue. All men are necessarily asking themselves and their world questions about the meaning of their own lives and their relationship to other people and the universe as a whole. These are primarily questions of meaning, and upon the answer to them depends their convictions as to whether life is or is not worth living, as to whether there is any significant moral dimension in human affairs.

Men do not ask these questions merely because they may happen to be endowed with a speculative turn of mind. They ask them because life asks them. They have really no choice. The very fact that they know an inward inconsistency between their own ideals and performance, and also an ambiguous and often confusing relationship to the forces of world affairs which impinge upon them, makes them demand some kind of meaningfulness in order to keep going.

Men ask religious questions because they are forced to ask them as part of living in an existential world. Traditional theological vocabularies, however, do not always appear to be very useful in phrasing their questions or in stating the answers they are seeking. Traditional symbols, in the broad sense, do not always seem to be genuine descriptions of the problems they know themselves to be facing. On the most fundamental level, our modern world does not know how to phrase its genuinely religious needs with any feeling of confidence in the traditions and symbols it has inherited.

Men must make sense out of life in order to keep living. The experience of the past half century has made it impossible for many people to take for granted the nineteenth century confidence that life was self-explanatory, provided one looked at it hard enough, or that life was reducible to a basic order, provided men tried hard enough.

There are three aspects of man's personality that demand satisfaction if life is to be tolerable. These three needs must be related both to man's inner drives and to the outward pressures upon him. These elemental needs of the human personality make the religious problem inevitable, and where they are taken sufficiently into account the significance of Archbishop Temple's statement is obvious. The three aspects are security, status, and achievement. Unless men achieve what they regard to be security, life cannot make sense. Unless they feel that they have an undeniable status of some kind in their scheme of things, life cannot be satisfactory. Unless men feel confident that their activity possesses some kind of self-authenticating value, life will always be confusing.

Security, to take the first, refers to the need felt by every human being for an impregnable citadel of safety at the heart of his being. Consciously, it can take a variety of forms — economic, social, physical, personal. A friend of mine used to tell me that the only thing he feared was " economic death." He was a self-made technical expert, whose gauge of the value of his activity lay in his ability to provide comfort and opportunity for his children, and this ability depended entirely upon his continued earning power. If anything should destroy that — an accident, ill-health or the loss of his job — life would just cease as far as its worth was concerned.

Security for most people refers above all to an inward awareness that there is someone else who cares. The average man needs to feels sure, to take for granted, that, regardless of what he does or what happens to him, he will be esteemed by someone else for his own sake. The security of being loved is a very obvious need in children, but no one outgrows it. Its frame of reference changes, but the need continues, and where it is not adequately met, no substitute can serve in its place.

Status, the second need, refers to man's aggressive relationship to the world, as distinguished from his defensive relationship. While people may differ widely as to the kind of status that is important — economic, social, technical, and the like — all men need to feel assured that they have a place which is theirs by right, by undeniable right, in the scheme of things. Regardless of what a man understands his status to be, he is shaken in a fundamental way by whatever profoundly questions it. Men can accept a good deal of serious criticism provided it does not appear to threaten their status. But when this vital need is threatened, even the mildest rebuff is desperately resisted.

Where status is involved, men and women will sacrifice many other values to protect it. In the functional sense, child sacrifice did not go out of fashion when the brazen images of Moloch at Tyre and Sidon were torn down. People still sacrifice their children to satisfy their own status needs. Many a woman seeks to fulfill her own social ambitions through her daughter, regardless of the daughter's own talents. Many a man is heedless of his son's natural capacities in his determination to promote his own status through the boy's powers. Many children die just as effectively at the altar of parental self-will as they once did to satisfy the demands of primitive cults.

Achievement, in the third place, refers most obviously to voca-tion. But achievement is by no means limited to the economics of earning a living or carrying on a home. For many people in the modern world, jobs are the means of financing life, while achievement satisfactions are sought elsewhere. The almost uni-versal problem of Western civilization today lurks in the area of achievement, cutting across lines of race and class and educa-tional background. Because of the way society is organized, most people have to spend a large part of their waking hours in some kind of organized enterprise which may be meaningless. And where men are denied a feeling that what they are doing with their lives is important, they are bankrupt at heart.

There are many mild alcoholics in all classes of society, for example, who are frustrated on the level of achievement. The money reward, even of a successful career, does not satisfy every-one's need for a full creative life. The charm and comfort which a woman may give her home, regardless of her economic re-sources, does not in itself guarantee that homemaking will con-tinue to be a meaningful occupation day after day, when so much of it is spent in repetitious chores. The world is filled with un-happy people who do not really believe their own intellectual statements about the importance of what they are doing. The world is filled with miscast men and women who do not know what to do, because they are financially dependent upon their jobs, and it takes a brave soul to sacrifice security in order to satisfy his achievement need. The world is filled with men and women who think they are miscast in their vocations, because they do not know how to interpret their activity in a way that gives them happiness. Many people in these conditions seek an outlet in alcohol or some other escape mechanism in order to compensate for a larger frustration.

The nature of these three drives prevents the possibility of their being satisfied by a policy of calculation. While people do weigh prospective actions in the light of their needs for security, status, and achievement, as they understand these needs, such consideration is actually concerned with details rather than with the total meaning. These three needs are expressions of the entire personality — including man's understanding of the meaning of his own life, his relationships with other people, and his place in the total scheme of things.

Since these three drives are aspects of human nature in operation, they can no more be denied than can the use of a man's digestive tract or his apparatus for breathing. Yet, unlike physical organs, which function almost automatically and do not interfere with one another save in disease, these three aspects of man's total being continually intrude upon consciousness, because of the very fact that they do get in one another's way. The complex structure of the human personality in operation makes it impossible for these demands to be satisfied automatically, although it is true that we are less conscious of them when everything is going smoothly than when we are under tension.

The life organized solely on the basis of security is always threatened by the status and achievement needs. We are seldom willing to let well enough alone. Anyone who has ever tried to reason with a child while disciplining him cannot but recall how the child's aggressive protest tends to complicate a bad situation, when it is obvious that the child would serve his own self-interest better by not protesting. But men cannot ignore their status needs, even when security may be endangered by affirming them. The baseball player who has just been called out by the umpire feels an inner compulsion to object, even though he knows the umpire cannot reverse himself, while he, the player, may get himself expelled from the field for his trouble.

In the same manner, man's need for a sense of achievement continually threatens his security. In perhaps an extreme way,

the answer of the mountain climber Mallory to those who asked
him why he continued to risk his life in such unprofitable and
dangerous enterprises as trying to climb Mount Everest illustrates the point. Mallory replied that the joy of achieving the impossible was its own reward; the thrill of the attempt was its own
satisfaction. And Mallory eventually lost his life demonstrating
his conviction.

Man's desire for status is also threatened by his need for security. One of the points illustrated again and again in *Lee's
Lieutenants,* the classic " study of command " by Douglas Southall
Freeman, is that the inner need for playing it safe and being sure
in advance of action was the greatest liability in an otherwise
competent officer. Many of Lee's officers found themselves unable
to make positive, aggressive decisions in a crisis. When the need
for security assumed sway, the men failed to meet their responsibilities.

Man's need for achievement can be prejudiced by his inner
demand for status. " Playing the gallery " often spoils the performance of otherwise capable athletes. And achievement can
easily be thwarted by the need for security where men hesitate
to depart from familiar routines in home or business because
they are used to doing things one way and they are not sure that
experiments will work. Thus, these needs do not automatically
harmonize with one another.

Regardless of the various areas in which men may look for
answers to the three elemental drives for security, status, and
achievement, the fact remains that the satisfaction of these drives
is the essence of the religious appetite. Since men and women
live in a world where these drives can never be completely or
permanently satisfied, even though they may be subdued to a
certain extent by spiritual anesthetics, they must continue to ask
questions about life's meaning.

The experiences we have encourage or threaten our understanding of what is necessary for security, status, and achievement. In other words, there are religious issues at the bottom of many human problems which are all too often regarded as merely economic, sociological, or psychiatric. Where threats to security, status, and achievement are involved, people must be enabled to make an interpretation of life's meaning that allows them to live with their problems, if they are going to be helped at all. And this is essentially a religious issue.

One of the great problems for clergymen and social workers during the depression was to take fully into account the fact that they were working with men whose faith had been destroyed — not simply their self-confidence, not simply their control over economic circumstances, nor their ability to find the kind of jobs for which they were trained. Since life's meaning had been measured by economic success, unemployment became the symptom not merely of the handicapped life but also of the meaningless, hopeless life. Under the circumstances, it was usually hard to make the resources of the churches serve any really practical purpose, because, regardless of whether or not the people concerned were church members, they understood life's meaning in terms quite unrelated to their appreciation of the Church. Yet the victims of the depression were very often facing basically religious problems, and they could not be aided successfully until they acquired a working interpretation of life which gave them a new perspective.

All of us are forced to make some kind of interpretation of experience to allow us to deal satisfactorily with the continual threats to our security, status, and achievement. These interpretations take the form of symbols — words, customs, actions — which make the interpretation dynamic. We do not deal creatively with living problems solely by intellectual descriptions of them. We have to interpret them in such a way as to live with them, and this is where symbols come in. The word " symbol " is often associated with the adjective "mere" — "mere symbol" — and in some situations this may be an apt expression. In the area of living religion, however, as in many associated areas of life involving relationships between people, symbols must be understood in a "sacramental" sense, as making possible an appreciation of reality that is not possible in any other way.

The use of the term "symbols" with reference to the deeper interpretations of experience points to the fact that all such interpretations, no matter how theoretically individualistic, are essentially social. They describe relationships between people, because it is in the course of interpersonal contact, either immediate or implied, that the threats to security, status, and achievement arise. A kiss is a good example of an action symbol which dramatizes dynamically the relationship between two people who can affirm or deny each other's needs in the areas of security, status, and achievement. Because a kiss can also be used perfunctorily, or even to betray, the further point is made that the value of symbols depends upon their actual use even more than upon the theories behind them.

One of the marks of civilization is the use of symbols to communicate meaning from heart to heart as well as from mind to mind. Symbols can be either words or acts or material things, provided the society that uses them shares to some significant degree an appreciation of what they are supposed to signify. A dollar bill would signify nothing to a Hottentot who had no contact with Western society, while to an American it symbolizes so much purchasing power, and people are willing to exchange such a piece of paper for goods and services. A handclasp is a symbol that is used to signify a good many different things, although the meaning is usually made clear by the setting.

The use and appreciation of symbols does not necessarily mean that they accomplish the desired result. A handclasp can mark sincere agreement to co-operate, or it can cover a stab in the back. Yet, by and large, Western society has discovered that there is no way by which people can convey meaning as well as information to one another except by the use of symbols, even though the symbols themselves may be abused or misunderstood.

Word symbols are common ways by which people show their relationship to one another. The passwords and ritual of fraternities and lodges are not to be understood by simply taking the spoken words literally but, rather, as symbols of the brotherhood which the members are supposed to feel toward fellow members.

This use of symbols is not quite the same as the appreciation of the emotional content of words as has been revealed by the study of general semantics, but it does have a connection. The semanticists have shown us that certain words tend to convey attitudes rather than clear understanding, so that problems are often confused by mistaking an emotionally loaded word for an objective statement of fact. The word " bureaucrat " is a good example. Word symbols have actually the opposite purpose — deliberately to convey meaning and feeling, as well as fact, between people who are able to share a common approach to problems.

Symbols, therefore, imply both the existence of some kind of society in which people can communicate meaning to one another, and also the existence of general problems, which are to be understood by that society in certain ways. People do not use symbols just for the fun of it, but because they have jobs to do. At the same time, even where people do have common tasks, they do not use symbols unless they feel a relationship to one another at the same time. The word symbols of the Christian faith presuppose the Christian Church as a fellowship, with a common understanding of life's meaning based upon the conviction that all men essentially face the same problems in everyday living, even though details may differ.

Where the symbols are applied to the perennial human problems of security, status, and achievement, they are being used religiously, regardless of what the users may think or say about their activity. All religions, not only Christianity, use word symbols to describe the significance of these perennial problems and to point out the direction in which answers are to be sought and to indicate the kind of solutions which may be hoped for.

Religion consists of asking and answering questions about life's meaning, so that we are able to make decisions in real life situations. Because experience is three-dimensional, involving depth as well as time and space, these questions and answers have to be expressed at least partly in symbolic terms in order to do justice to the problems involved. Part of the confusion of our times is the result of many people's trying to describe experience in what they believed to be a scientific way without recognizing that in the transition from the laboratory to the market place they also moved from the world of the two-dimensional to the three-dimensional.

The most basic religious question is, *Who am I?* and its answer involves one's appreciation of God, man, and the universe. Everyone has to ask this question and to live by some sort of answer. The Behaviorists who try to reduce human problems to electrical and mechanical engineering have to ask the question and live by the answer they think they find. The Communists are trying to do it. The "Peace of Mind" parody of Christianity is trying also. So is every other group that tries to deal with man's fundamental problems.

The second question is, *Where did I come from and where am I going?* This is really an enlargement on the first question, asked so as to take account of the fact that life is an ongoing process no matter how one looks at it. The third question is simply, *Why?* Is there any purpose to the process in which I am involved, through which I am somehow related to the experiences of other people?

Christianity offers a way of asking all three questions so that one is forced to face facts about himself as well as to recognize the realities of outside circumstance. And Christianity provides an answer that is not so much a set of propositions, a systematic structure of theories, as it is a dynamic way of living — with God and with each other.

When we recognize that Christianity on this level is engaged in the same process as all other religions — claiming to make it possible for men to ask and find an answer to life's basic questions and so deal adequately with the continual threats to security, status, and achievement — we need to add a major qualification. To be sure, Christianity is in competition with the other religions of the world, both those which claim to be religions and those which simply act that way. But the choice between Christianity and its possible alternatives is not on the basis that the Christian approach is more sweetly reasonable than the others. While Christianity does make it possible to ask the questions and to receive the answers, its approach is one that people will not want to use unless something has revolutionized their way of looking at life. At first encounter, and even more so on thorough acquaintance, the Christian approach is a scandal and offense, as Paul knew when he wrote, "But we preach Christ crucified, to the Jews a stumblingblock, and to the Greeks foolishness, but to them that are called, both Jews and Greeks, Christ the power of God and the wisdom of God."

Whether religion, as far as content is concerned, is traditional or spontaneous or merely a reflection of the cultural climate, its vitality depends upon its adequacy for answering man's questions about life's meaning for himself. Where Christianity as the great tradition of Western civilization is concerned, the issue is first of all whether men and women today are really able to handle their security, status, and achievement problems by means of Christian symbols or whether the attempt to use the Christian tradition to understand their problems confuses the issue.

Behind the theoretical pictures given in the Christian tradition of God, man, and the universe is the fact that these pictures purport to make it possible for men and women to understand themselves, their relationships to other people, and their response to the pressures of the world, in a creative manner. The Christian tradition claims to provide a basis for handling the problems of security, status, and achievement that is more realistic and more workable than any other. But men and women will accept this only through finding that it meets the tests of real experience.

If Christianity is to become a vital force in the modern world, it must provide a language in which men may phrase their deepest questions. It must make possible the statement of these problems more clearly in Christian terms than in any other tongue. This test has nothing to do with demonstrating the accuracy of objective theories. The proof consists in affording the basis by which men understand their problems as they try to deal with them.

If a man has to put storm windows on his house, he has to use some kind of tool to drive the screws. He can use a kitchen knife, a nail file, a pair of scissors, or in an extreme emergency, a dime. Most of us have discovered, however, that the best instrument for driving a screw is a screw driver. But putting on the storm windows is not an elective. One has no choice here. The only choice lies in the instrument chosen for the job. And wisdom prompts a man to select the device that works the best.

Is the situation with regard to religion any different? The religions men use are the tools they happen to have selected to satisfy their needs for security, status, and achievement in a world where these elemental drives threaten each other and are continually threatened by circumstance. Real men have to live in a real world. The task of living calls for the use of some tool by the use of which experience may be interpreted. Religion is, in this sense, the master tool for dealing with life, and men use the tool that appears to do the job as they understand it. This is no argument in favor of pragmatism, but rather a plain observation of what happens in human life.

When we recognize the functional nature of Christianity as a religion, we must also face the fact that few people, if any, ever become Christians by the road of comparative religion alone — looking over the alternatives and then choosing between them. Christianity is *a* religion in the way it works, but it must be *the* religion for those who would make sense out of life in its terms.

CHAPTER III

Death and Guilt

RELIGIOUS questions continually recur. We cannot make sense out of life and then freeze it, and expect it to remain frozen. Since the questions and answers really arise out of our fundamental need to appreciate the full significance of our experience in a world where circumstances are always changing, our religious understandings must take this into account.

Our appreciation of life changes from day to day and from moment to moment. This is due partly to the changes in external situations, and partly to the somewhat mysterious inner drives of our own personalities. People find a zest for life and then lose it, and then sometimes recover it again. People are "converted" to a new point of view, and then drop back into the old patterns. Therefore, any religious approach to fundamental problems must be dynamic if it is to serve its purpose.

Man's religious questions grow out of his natural need to find an adequate security, status, and sense of achievement. But these three essentials for meaningful living are themselves continually changing — both as to what they seem to demand and as to what appears to satisfy them. They are at the mercy of man's own inner psychological pressures, which disregard the laws of logic and the canons of expediency, and they are also at the mercy of external events. "The best-laid schemes o' mice an' men gang aft agley."

The process of living by faith, regardless of the particular faith, involves living in a changing world where time is real. New tests of faith, which can never be foreseen completely, arise. Our understandings and appreciations of what makes life meaningful are never safe from possible threats. As James Russell Lowell understood it:

> "New occasions teach new duties;
> Time makes ancient good uncouth;
> They must upward still, and onward,
> Who would keep abreast of Truth."

We change, and the very process of biological and sociological maturing makes every accomplishment in the areas of security, status, and achievement tentative. The world around us changes. Parents, who have worked out adequate relationships with their preschool children and allowed for their growth within the safe limitations of a home-dominated world, discover that the new world of the school-age child requires a rethinking of patterns. To try to continue what worked well enough with four-year-olds will cause endless confusion with six-year-olds; while the parents, particularly of the first child, have no guarantee in advance that they will be able to meet the new test.

External forces vary in their impact upon us. Security, status, and achievement patterns that could be taken for granted before the depression of the thirties were badly shaken when the financial collapse occurred. Understandings that can be counted on in peacetime frequently fail to be as satisfying in wartime. Status patterns of wartime origin are sometimes badly threatened by the advent of peace when officers who have had an assured position in the armed forces have to return to civilian living without any such assurance.

Because we live in a changing world, our religion, to be adequate, must be sufficiently dynamic to allow us to move on from old circumstances and to relate ourselves to new situations. Yet we must still be ourselves in the process. We can never live today in terms of what was satisfactory yesterday, nor can we count on what we take for granted today as sufficing for tomorrow. If we ignore these facts, we are doomed to hopeless and endless confusion. But at the same time we cannot merely let ourselves drift, although some people try to do so. We are at heart the same persons who faced yesterday's problems and who will also face tomorrow's issues; and to drift in a kind of psychological opportunism is to be less than ourselves. We know this to be true.

Since our security, status, and achievement are needs that are rooted in the very nature of existence, our religious questions and answers must be relevant if they are to be usable. Yet, since we live in a changing world, religious issues can never be settled and "put on ice.'" They will reappear in new forms in new situations.

Religious questions are involved in every transition a man or a woman has to make in the course of a normal life: from infant to school child; from elementary school to the more self-consciously one-generation world of youth; from high school to the freedom and opportunity of college; from college to choosing a job; changing jobs; getting married; becoming a parent; having one's children get married; facing retirement and old age oneself. Religious issues are likewise involved in every change brought about by political, economic, and social forces to the extent that these influence the setting and activity of our lives.

All other answers to life's questions depend upon the adequacy of our religion. When our religious understanding is threatened in any serious way, relatively routine adjustments, such as details of home management or business, become occasions for confusion or fear. Where the prevailing religion of society no longer seems to enable men and women to deal with their real problems, that society and its institutions become unstable.

We have to take seriously the fact that we live in a changing world. In other words, time is a real factor in our understanding of our own experience. The hands of the clock continue to move, but in one direction only, and the passing moments spell the end of old relationships and the birth of new ones. Unless men come to terms with the facts — that historical changes continue to occur in every area of human activity just because time keeps passing — they cannot live satisfying lives. Their security, status, and achievement will always be in danger. Indeed, they cannot be themselves.

The fact of time keeps the religious issue continually alive, because time involves change toward both the future and the past. The fact of time, therefore, continually threatens the bases for security, status, and achievement that men have worked out. Satisfactory relationships, even if attained, cannot last forever. They become obsolete and irrelevant and often destructive. At the same time, the inadequacies in past relationships have a way of persisting and continuing to threaten security, status, and achievement.

The effect of time is double — in relationship to the future and to the past. *The symbol for the threat of the future is death. The symbol for the threat of the past is guilt.* Death and guilt together make up the continual threat which men feel, whether appreciated consciously or known only as a haunting anxiety, in every serious decision arising in connection with practical affairs. Death and guilt together are the double threat that hangs over every satisfaction attained as regards security, status, and achievement. Death and guilt are at the root of man's religious need, and except where they are dealt with functionally and adequately no religious expression can satisfy people very long.

Every person who is fully conscious is intellectually aware that he will die some day. Yet, while the fact is certain, the hour is uncertain and the meaning of the experience defies comprehension. For this reason death has a religious meaning as the symbol for the threatening future. We know change to be real and time relentless. We know today's satisfactions cannot last forever. Nevertheless, we can find no guarantees for the future.

The term "death" is used in this volume in a specialized sense — but its symbolic meaning is definitely related to the way in which men face practical questions in an uncertain world. Death as a religious symbol is, therefore, derived from death as a psychological problem.

Every known religion says something about the meaning of death, because it is so profoundly related to man's need to make sense out of life. The funeral customs of different cultures reflect their answers to the unavoidable problem of living in a world where men die physically and also of living in a world where the outcome of human actions is uncertain. The survival of soothsayers, fortunetellers, and astrologers in a sophisticated culture shows that men are not only curious about the future, but that they have an inner need to come to terms with life in a world where the future always tends to threaten the present.

Death is the symbol for the threat of the future. The future is always uncertain. It can never be known in advance with any assurance that it will turn out as expected. It may be worse; it may be better; but the future always and necessarily involves change. It involves new adjustments. It involves at least some revision in the way men seek to satisfy their needs for security, status, and achievement. And there can never be any guaranty that the result will be adequate.

Every transition in normal life involves the problem of death. The inevitable physical decease, which everyone faces sooner or later, is not the real religious problem. Its inevitability and unknowable meaning, however, serve to highlight the significance of the more immediate transitions men encounter. In actual life "little deaths" raise more serious threats to meaningfulness than physical decease. It is when men and women face actual problems of decision, which threaten their security, status, and achievement, that death is a religious and psychological issue.

Every normal transition in life involves death, and when we refuse to "die" in this sense, our lives become not so much tragic as ridiculous. The middle-aged sorority sister is an example. When she carried the daisies or planted the ivy or was an attendant to the Queen of the May, no doubt she could find life's satisfactions chiefly in the area of youthful romance. Yet there are many women who have found no richer and fuller basis for satisfying living in their maturity, because they have not dared to let go what was once so fulfilling. Or take the superannuated boy scout, who at the age of forty-five has all the freshness, the enthusiasm, the boyish charm, and the complete lack of stick-to-itiveness of a thirteen-year-old. Because he cannot die to adolescence, he cannot adequately meet the demands of husbandhood and parenthood.

Every marriage involves the issue of death to such an extent that only when people truly "die" can their marriage be complete. The average boy or girl in the early twenties has the greatest individual self-sufficiency that he will ever have. His formal education is completed, or the end, at least, is in sight. He can usually spend his money as he pleases, and associate with whom he pleases without having to account to anybody. Marriage requires that two young people voluntarily "die" to this independence in order to be reborn as partners, with only the promise — not really any assurance — that rebirth will be possible.

Having our children grow up is a succession of deaths. When we first learn, sometimes by the half-caught remark, that they know the facts of life — and not always in too pretty a manner — something happens to us. When they claim the right to make their own plans without taking parents into account, something happens to us — and it happens each time this growing up affects a new area of life. When they want to get married, and we know we cannot choose their partners for them, and also that we must let them go out into the world of their own which we can never fully share, we die again.

To move from one community to another involves death. One abandons the neighborhood where people and facilities are familiar in the hope, but with no guaranty, that the change will work out for the best. Many families who have had to move to a new home in another state have found themselves caught in a meaningless existence, because they are not willing to let go their old ties in order to accept new ones. Every holiday finds them going back to " Kentucky." Every friendship is thought of in terms of the old " home town."

To change one's job involves death. Not only transitions but, even more, decisions, which may or may not be in connection with the normal changes of maturity, raise the threat. Before one can make a decision — about a new job, or about anything else that is important — he has several possibilities open to him, as well as the situation in which he happens to be. More often than not some kind of decision is forced by events — a man has to choose some kind of job; he has to live somewhere; he has to have some associations, just in order to keep going. But, in any event, every decision involves the killing of the other possibilities to a large extent, and every significant decision involves the death of the old order of living.

The significance of death for religion is that men are driven to find some interpretation of life's meaning that will give them a basis for security, status, and achievement, while they can never be assured that the new situations into which they are forced by the forward movement of time will allow that interpretation to remain useful. Therefore, every change involves the threat of death, and many involve the fact of death. To live in a changing world requires some kind of faith, which will make some specific allowance for this problem, if life is to be meaningful. Death itself can never be eliminated as a threat.

The symbol of death is also applicable to social situations. One major element in industrial conflict during the past century has been the failure, perhaps more obviously on the management side but to a real extent on the union side, to accept the realities of new situations, where adjustments have to be worked out on new bases. Worker-management councils might be accepted in some industries as a wartime necessity, but few concerns have been experimental enough to seek for a new and broader-base approach to policy-making.

On the level of municipal government, the major metropolitan areas of the United States are caught in a web of circumstance resulting from the fact that institutions that once had a practical usefulness, such as county and township systems, do not die readily when situations call for it. Therefore, real needs in the fields of education, sanitation, police and fire protection, and transportation are inadequately met in many communities.

Probably the most obvious social application of the problem to which the symbol of death applies is in the area of international relations. National sovereignty served a real purpose in the days when the great middle class was breaking the chains of the feudal system and when first commercial development and then the industrial revolution brought new capacities to the people of many countries. In our day, the fact that national sovereignty is not seriously qualified by the major countries of the world results in tragedy. In American history this has been the cause for a series of irresponsible actions which have had world-wide consequences, and the ambiguities of the picture confuse our relationship to the United Nations today.

Guilt is the religious symbol for the threat of the past. As in the case of death, the term is used deliberately in a specialized sense, but the meaning is definitely related to the way in which men feel about their experience. No person can honestly survey his own past activities and relationships with unmingled satisfaction. In one way or another, all men are aware that they have failed to do justice to the opportunities and associations they have had. The results of these past failures of omission and commission continue to plague them, no matter how much they may rationalize their actions or try to pass the blame to others.

The child's desire for punishment, which survives in adult life, is the psychological expression of his desire somehow to erase the effect of the past so that it will no longer threaten the present. Nearly every systematic theory of religion has some kind of idea of atonement — whether it be merely one of renewed moral effort or one of restoration to a broken fellowship. Every sensitive person is aware that the most poignant human problems are of human origin. Every honest person is aware, regardless of his philosophy, that he has contributed both to the difficulties of others and to the confusion of his own life. To use the term " guilt " is, therefore, no exaggeration of the way men feel. Although people may vary in the intensity of their awareness, and although their moods may change with changing situations, everyone knows what the word means.

When the term " guilt " is used, it is in a general rather than a psychopathic sense, although what is said may apply more or less to problems of psychopathology as well as to normal living. Every change, every transition, every decision faces us with the threats of our past errors, mistakes, and failures. Because we have incompletely sensed previous problems, and inadequately responded to previous challenges, and because we have not measured up to previous responsibilities, our ability to find a satisfactory security, status, and achievement basis is always problematical. And even as we attain some kind of satisfaction for these elemental needs, we are haunted by the memory of the past.

Since it is not within man's capacity to understand the full

import of the situations in which he is involved, or to make any
decision with absolute and unqualified virtue, or to have at his
command unlimited power to handle all the angles, man is never
in a position where he can be completely satisfied with the effect of his own past upon his own present — unless he deliberately misreads the evidence. Indeed, if he is at all sensitive, he
knows that his own mistakes, errors, and failures have contributed partly to the problems he now faces.

What is past is past. Guilt, in this sense, is our awareness that
we cannot undo the mistakes, the wrong decisions, the egotistical
choices, the inaccurate estimates we once have made. We cannot
undo what we have done as if it had never been done in the first
place. Sometimes we can make amends. Sometimes we can learn
from experience. Sometimes things turn out for the best anyhow.
But we cannot, if we are over twenty-one years of age, relive the
years under twenty-one and handle our opportunities differently.
As we face transitions today, and as we try to make the decisions
life forces upon us, we do so in the awareness, consciously or
unconsciously, that we have a cumulative problem to deal with
and that we shall continue to add to it.

In no place is the meaning of guilt, as related to the past,
clearer than in the case of bereavement. In such situations it is
the problem of guilt which so often provides the cutting edge of
sorrow. What hurts people is that the kindness which should
have been done can no longer be done. The apology which ought
to have been made can no longer be made. The letter which
should have been written; the errand which could have been so
easily undertaken — nothing can be done about them as far as
the specific relationship to the deceased person is concerned.
What is past is past.

Any religion, therefore, that is to serve men as a vital interpretation of life's meaning in a world of dynamic circumstances
must have something real to say to the problem of guilt. Man's

sense of need on this level is just as real as his need on the level of death. In one way or another both are rooted deep in the heart of every living person, although some may understand their problems better under one heading than under the other. In any event, the problem of guilt is real.

Guilt as a symbol is also capable of social application just as in the case of the symbol of death. It may take the form of national neurosis brought about by the disclosure of half-concealed social immoralities. It is hard to apply the symbol of guilt adequately to other countries, but modern French history seems to reflect a serious element of guilt from the time of the Dreyfus affair, through the Stavisky scandal, and then in the Vichy regime, and the problem dogs the footsteps of the Government even today. There certainly was a wide-scale guilt reaction in Germany after World War II, and the denials of guilt in the resurgent nationalism of the early 1930's, denials which may be repeated in the near future, suggest the presence of what is being denied.

Guilt as a social phenomenon has been noticeable in the reaction of a great many conscientious people in the United States to the knowledge that this country not only developed but used the first atomic bomb. Many prominent physicists reacted to this fact in a public manner. Possibly some of the confusion in the public mind as to when the use of atomic weapons is proper can be traced to an unsolved sense of social guilt which makes it difficult to clarify the issues in a world where atomic science is one of the actualities.

Death and guilt are aspects of the raw stuff of life. They are inescapably connected with living. Every time a man looks at his watch he is shown that time is moving on, and it never moves backward. The future is always pressing in upon us, with its unknowable demands requiring the death of today's satisfactions and understandings, while the past continues as a reality, with its ineradicable record of mistakes made and failures met. Every watch is a parable of man's basic religious need as he tries to make sense out of life.

In the last chapter we saw that everyone has to find some way of handling his perennial need for security, status, and achievement. The symbols of death and guilt point to the fact that there is no permanent way of dealing with these needs that will prevent their recurrence as problems. The fact of change involves new decisions which have to be made, and every decision carries with it a threat to what we take to be the way of handling our needs for security, status, and achievement. The symbols of death and guilt describe the profound nature of this threat. The fact of time's movement forward, the concomitant of change, guarantees that new problems will arise for us to deal with as individuals and in society, and this makes any permanent solution to the problems of security, status, and achievement impossible.

Only a religion that appears to deal adequately with the problems of death and guilt as men happen to understand them will ever be used to meet the functional demands of religion in living. Only a religion that continues to be adequate as the means of understanding and handling new threats as they are brought about by changing situations, transitions, and decisions will ever remain vital. Yet, if men are to live and find life meaningful, they must have a faith that is able to withstand all the threats of death and guilt that may occur, without falsifying reality and without omitting significant problems. As a matter of fact, the faith of every man and the prevailing religious understanding of every society is continually subjected to the tests of adequacy on this most important of functional levels, and ultimately every faith must come to terms somehow with their reality.

The word "faith" has been used several times, and should be defined. In the setting of the functional interpretation of religion, *faith is that combination of understanding and confidence upon which a person acts when he must make real decisions.* When a young man and young woman are thinking of getting married, neither can foresee the details of the future. Neither can be sure he will be able to rise above the habit patterns acquired during his lifetime, which may interfere with his being fully accepted by his partner. The young couple presumably use their best intelligence, and try to take into account all the angles to marriage — their congeniality with each other, their economic prospects, their other responsibilities, their respective hopes and ambitions. But since life is the way it is, they cannot wait until all the answers are in before acting. Using a combination of what they think they understand and what they believe to be meaningful, they act anyhow.

In other words, everyone lives by faith of some kind, since faith is the basis upon which everyone acts when faced with a decision involving the threats of death and guilt. For the young couple getting married, death is the real issue — a new and unknown life lies ahead, while the familiar patterns of single self-completeness must be largely abandoned. For the young couple, also, guilt is real, since neither can approach marriage as a blank sheet of paper, but only as a person who has had about twenty years or more of trial and error, success and failure, understanding and misunderstanding. In marriage, and in every other significant crisis, life demands some kind of action, and action is only possible on the basis of some kind of faith.

The test of faith is not whether people are enabled, or not enabled, to act. It is what kind of action they find themselves enabled to make. Where life is being appreciated accurately, action must necessarily include not only immediate responses to immediate stimuli, but the total meaning of what is involved for the people concerned. The question is not whether death and guilt are being met, since they cannot be avoided. The question is whether they are being met in terms of an adequate religion, so that the action involved — a marriage, a business decision, a parent and child problem, or whatever it is — is as fully meaningful in its totality as possible.

In the final analysis, the consideration of the meaning of faith in the light of death and guilt raises the question of freedom in its most profound sense. Freedom is generally understood as referring to the absence of controls over one's possible actions. There can be no freedom, however, in this sense from the fact of time — change occurs and with it men and women have to make transitions, whether they like it or not. Decisions are forced on them of such a character that even an attempted evasion becomes itself a kind of decision. Freedom may be understood as referring to the possibility of choosing between alternatives — in the sense that in the United States men have a free choice at the polls and can vote for whom they desire, even though they know that any practical choice is limited to one of two candidates in most situations. Freedom to choose between possible courses of action may be very nice to have and, indeed, may be very valuable in certain circumstances, but by itself it does not contribute much to make life meaningful.

When it is realized, however, that every significant act is an act of faith, freedom can be understood to refer to something more basic, something which does make life meaningful. *The free act, religiously speaking, is that which a man is enabled to make because he has come to grips adequately with the problems of death and guilt.* Hence he can act without being defeated in advance by the past, even though he has made false choices and evaded responsibility and the historical consequences of the past acts cannot be erased. Although what has happened has happened, life can still be meaningful. He can also act without fearing the future, even though he cannot foresee it with any assurance, and nothing can be guaranteed in advance.

All religions are really attempts to combine faith and freedom for living men and women, because only such a combination endows life with undeniable meaningfulness. All religions have their own ways of trying to deal with the problems of death and guilt, no matter what names they may give to these problems. The real point is that if men are to have satisfying, meaningful lives, they must have an inner assurance of freedom — the confidence that what they do in present actions and relationships really counts. If they are to have this, they must understand their security, status, and achievement in such a way that they are, at one and the same time, able to meet the real demands of the real world and live with themselves.

CHAPTER IV

Meeting Life's Demand

THE religions men live by are the result of their encounter with the real world. No one ever thought up a hypothetical faith in an ivory tower and then went out into the world to see if it was a good fit. But all of us try to think through what we are doing and why in the light of our experience so that what we do and think in one area of life gears into what we think and do in other areas.

Men construct their religious interpretations in the process of meeting the real needs of their own human natures in the context of responding to the pressures of the world around them. People do not choose between various proposed theories about man and the universe as they might select between items of merchandise for sale. Instead, they encounter problems in real life and attempt to deal with them by using the resources they find available.

People may be brought up to subscribe verbally to the official opinions of some religious institution, and they may come to think of the term " religion " as referring to their affiliation with some organization. Likewise, people may be brought up to think of " religion " primarily as an ethical code which they ought to apply to life directly. But the religion they live by, whether or not they use the term, has become theirs by a more dynamic process than indoctrination. It has been the way by which they have felt it possible to attain and maintain security, status, and a sense of achievement in an uncertain world.

If Christianity is really to be *the* religion with convincing power, it has to provide the way by which real people meet the problems of a real world. "Making decisions for Jesus Christ" can have no serious religious meaning if it does not refer to making continual decisions in terms of Christian faith as we encounter the many demands and tests of home and office and community, which involve actual relationships with other people who are also trying to make their own decisions at the same time. Unless in some sense the experience of Brother Lawrence, who found God's presence in the kitchen as he polished pots and pans, can be ours in our daily work, the Christian faith will not be the religion by which we live.

People encounter various demands in everyday life. Because the demands exist, we have to do something about them. Trying to suppress them is just one possible way among others. Trying to ignore them is another. Whether or not these demands arise from our physiological and psychological structure, such as the desire for self-preservation or the drive to fulfill oneself in meaningful relations with a person of the opposite sex, or whether these demands are given by our culture, we still have to do something about them. Religions become vital by serving as the bases on which men interpret these demands to themselves and try to meet them.

Men and women encounter the threat of death in the course of recognizing some demand which may upset their patterns for security, status, and achievement. The psychological and biological pressures of adolescence, for instance, force teen-age boys and girls to do something about developing relationships with the opposite sex and discovering for themselves the meaning of adulthood. The demands are given by the very nature of things, even though they are channeled by prevailing social customs. No matter whether they welcome social contacts with the opposite sex or are afraid of them, they have to do something about the demand. No matter whether they want to assume adult responsibilities or not, they have to come to terms somehow with the adult world. For boys, the Selective Service law makes this both obvious and unavoidable.

In Western civilization, every young man and woman has to make decisions in connection with the complexities of his or her education. Something has to be done about economic independence. A vocation has to be selected. Relationships with parents have to be redefined. In a monogamous culture, young adulthood involves the process of selecting a single mate, and relations with the opposite sex involve not only pleasant associations of the moment but also selection of a lifelong partner. The problem of death is encountered as these decisions are made, and religious issues are raised, although people may not call them that.

The problem of guilt is likewise encountered in practical everyday life. When men and women are forced to make decisions, their difficulty is not only a matter of the unknowable future, but also an awareness of failure in the past. Psychopathic guilt illustrates the problem in exaggerated form, since the inability of sufferers to come to terms with the demands of real life may be the result of harking back to an imaginary past. But even psychopathic guilt had an original contact with reality in some actual transition or decision the sufferer was for some reason unable to meet. And since failure, whether real or imaginary, can never be accepted as the norm, our awareness of past errors, mistakes, and misjudgments suggests blame for somebody — ourselves, in spite of rationalizations.

For most people new situations raise questions recalling past experience, not simply as remembered fact, but also as judgment upon themselves. Since no one has ever responded perfectly to all the demands he has met, every new demand questions his ability to respond without endangering his own security, status, and achievement in the process. The process of marriage, no matter how delightful it may seem and how desirable one's proposed partner may appear, cannot but make one wonder whether he will find it meaningful. It is not only a question of an unknown future but also the fact that one remembers his previous associations with those of the other sex. Sometimes men and women may worry because they feel they are not quite worthy of the role of married person. Sometimes they may be concerned lest the causes for the breaking of previous attachments recur. Everyone with any experience knows that personal attraction does not necessarily lead to lasting companionship or guarantee a changed personality for himself.

In other words, men must live religiously if they are to live at all, because they continue to meet demands in the course of daily living that raise the questions of death and guilt. Since religion is the interpretation of life that makes possible the meeting of the demands and the making of decisions, religious issues recur in every new situation. Men can never escape the questions of death and guilt arising from life's pressures, although they may misunderstand them, deliberately distort them, or try to ignore them. These questions are encountered in connection with the real demands of the real world, because that is the way life works.

Culture cannot dispose of the problem. It cannot serve as an adequate substitute for religion, although all cultures are concerned with these problems. In the last analysis, living men and women in a real world may take for granted intellectually the prevailing theories about life that are current in their society, but every single individual puts these theories to the test himself, whether he knows what he is doing or not. But he may not be able to provide an adequate faith for himself when the prevailing theories are found wanting.

In Western culture, success has been regarded as the key to the satisfying life, and success has usually been defined in financial terms. The men and women who have attained what they regard as success — whether financial or social or in terms of popularity — like to think of their lives as relatively complete, and they are encouraged to think them so. Whenever the turn of fortune's wheel destroys or threatens success, or makes the attainment impossible, then life becomes meaningless. Those who jumped from office building windows after the stock market crash of 1929 did so because their religion had collapsed along with their bank accounts.

The pressures of death and guilt have to be met somehow or life ceases to be worth living. This is not a philosophical problem, even though it can provide thought for philosophers. For the average person, it is enough to have his own life and his more immediate relationships operating more or less smoothly. In other words, every person must have a religion that enables him to meet those demands, arising from his own inner nature and from the pressure of the outer world, which raise the problems of death and guilt and threaten him with meaninglessness.

Life's demands, however, are seldom clear and simple. Even when some aspects seem obvious, the total picture never is. The demands are often difficult to clarify, and more often than not they are in conflict with one another. For the average man, business represents a demand with which he must come to terms or die, since failure to meet the demand adequately may lead to unemployment and physical suffering for himself and for those dependent upon him, and also to the feeling that he himself is worthless. But he does not live in a world where he can solve his problem of meaningful living solely by trying to do the best he can in meeting the demand of business. The demand of his family may conflict with it, and the demand of family life —

whether or not he has a mature understanding of what the family can mean — is deeply related to his attainment of security, status, and achievement.

Many men fail to find their jobs fully satisfying as far as achievement is concerned, and they often turn to some hobby to supply what is lacking. But the hobby may conflict with the real demands of business and possibly with those of the family. For other people, the demand of the community in the form of social service activity must be included in the pattern of a full and meaningful life, making possible a three-way or even a four-way conflict.

Many people never seem to find a meaningful response to the demands of business and family. Even though substitute satisfactions may be found in other areas to give needed security, status, and achievement, the original demands continue. Because they are usually functional in the sense of supplying " bread and butter " or the maintenance of a home, they cannot be ignored, even though they do not seem to be meaningful. They are necessarily time-consuming and attention-consuming, and something has to be done about them. This may take the form of alcohol or gambling, and these in turn may form still other demands with which men must come to terms.

The pattern of conflicting demands is also found in the group structure of the world. The class pattern of society originates in the functional breakdown involved in supplying goods and services, since not everyone can do every job, either by knowing how or through administrative efficiency. There have to be distinctions in the personnel in factories, stores, and public services. But it is only natural that the people who make up these industrial groupings understand the demand of business primarily in terms of their own relationship to the process and, consequently, tend to resist the activity of those who are related from " the other end of the stick." Society, which needs goods and services, finds itself in a conflict of demands, and is subjected to interpretations and propaganda reflecting special interests rather than the objective situation. When a vital industry, such as coal, is on strike, this problem forces people, as third parties to the dispute, to make what amounts to religious decisions.

Political life reflects the conflict of demands. To be aware of the conflict at all is usually to be related to it directly. More often than not it takes the form of the conflict of my group with some other group, my nation with another nation. In any event, political reality tends to create conflict between us and those who are differently related to the same demand. It is impossible for an American to view the tension with Russia objectively, no matter how liberal he thinks himself to be. Even if he should take a pro-Communist stand, he does so as an American who believes that his understanding is the solution to a conflict. He cannot intelligently deny the existence of the problem.

When men understand the demands laid upon them by the conflicting nature of their own relationships to other people and their own needs for security, status, and achievement, and also by other people's needs for security, status, and achievement, they cannot help realizing that they are "divided men in a divided world." It is in the process of trying to make sense out of this problem that men understand God. In the last analysis, their appreciation of God is the religious expression of what to do about conflicting demands — what to do in conformance with reality.

Polytheism, the worship of many gods, is not just an expression of primitive fancy. It is a description of man's feeling that nothing can be done to unify life's demands and eliminate the conflict. The only alternative is to mitigate the result in one's own experience. The gods of the Greco-Roman Pantheon were always fighting with one another as the very natural picture of a world in which there was no reconciliation possible between the demands of wisdom, for instance, and those of war.

Modern men have outgrown simple polytheism. Very few people in Western civilization believe in a multitude of deities. Everyone subscribes intellectually to belief in one God if he believes in any. In other words, few people hold seriously to the view of life that sees no solution to the internal and external conflicts which continually raise the problems of guilt and death. But while men may believe in some kind of theoretical solution to the problem, they generally live by one of two basic attitudes — alternating between them, with one or the other tending to predominate.

When men face the task of making sense out of life, safeguarding security, status, and achievement in a world of conflicting demands, they may regard the ultimate solution as purely theoretical. When they see the task this way, they feel that little can be done about it in everyday experience. All of us have moods when we feel that the only way to make life tolerable is to avoid issues as far as possible and let ourselves be carried along by the tide of circumstance. Perhaps such a way of living may not be ideal, but in a far from ideal world it seems practical at times. In other words, the easiest way to handle the problems of guilt and death often appears to be one of refusing to worry about the moral implications of our actions any more than absolutely necessary, while adjusting to whatever demands are laid upon us.

With all that can be said in favor of the advantages of modern suburban life, behind a lot of it is the attitude that the best way to meet the demands of a confusing world is to do one's best to avoid as many of them as possible. People avoid many social issues by the expedient of living in communities that are insulated for them, but the question remains as to whether they live in a real world. Professor Rosenstock-Huessy of Dartmouth has made an interesting analysis of this attitude in his book *The Christian Future.*

On the other hand, men also feel that by an aggressive handling of the problem of daily life the whole issue of conflict can be overcome. We have moods when we feel sure that a rigid maintenance of some kind of standard, an unswerving loyalty to principles, would solve the problem of meaningful living. If all men could be led to build their individual and social lives on some such basis, the problems of guilt and death would no longer perplex us. In other words, the issue appears then to be one of denying the importance of adjustment to changing circumstance, but standing rigidly for a strong moral code.

In the history of Christianity from the earliest days down to the present, there has been a tendency for little groups to separate from the larger fellowship because of their desire to maintain a more rigid moral code. Some of the early Gnostics in the days of Paul, the Donatists in the days of Augustine, the monastic movement to some extent, and, certainly, the little heretical sects of the Middle Ages, and some of the " Holiness " cults today are all built upon the belief that the members can live purer, more complete lives within the sect, and by aggressive conformance solve their problems. And again one has to ask whether these cults live in a real world.

The first type of response — living from day to day with as few questions as possible — is that of the Sadducee. The second type of response — living by formula — is that of the Pharisee. The two names are selected to describe the two basic religious attitudes in all men, because each was at one time in history given a highly systematic development and made the official program of a group approach to life. Each made genuine contributions to the religious development of mankind. Each left its mark on the Christian tradition — in the Scriptures which enshrine it, in adaptation to it, and in the problems Jesus had to face in working out his own faith.

The Sadducee and Pharisee are used here as type attitudes of the general human answer to death and guilt, rather than as systems that people live by today. Every living man has his Sadducee side and his Pharisee side, and while he may express one more than the other, he knows both at first hand.

The Sadducee always tries to concentrate solely on the problem of death and ignore that of guilt. By his solution of the problem of death in life's actual problems, he eliminates guilt as a significant issue. The Sadducee makes a tolerable adjustment to life today, eliminating unnecessary involvements — the sensible way to live. He thinks of peace for himself and quiet in the community. He does not want himself or the community bothered more than necessary, and he resents disorderly thought and action very deeply.

In the New Testament, the Sadducees were the official governing clique in Palestine, who held their power by compromise with the Romans. They were permitted to remain in control as long as they were able to keep the situation quiet. Their own justification, and it was not simply a rationalization of self-interest, was that by getting along with the Romans they enabled the Jews to maintain greater local autonomy and certainly larger cultural self-determination than any other subject people.

In the New Testament, both in their attempt to trip Jesus with a trick question and in Paul's attempt to divide his enemies after his final arrest, the Sadducees are described as denying the resurrection — any resurrection. In other words, they are described as acknowledging no ultimate moral criterion; by adjustment, compromise, getting along with the least possible trouble, they seek a life with as few unsettling questions as any man can have. To accept other questions as religiously germane is to submit oneself to judgment in one's own heart as to whether or not one has lived by the standard. To deny any resurrection is to deny the meaningfulness of the problem of guilt in any practical sense.

The Sadducee approach to life is shown very clearly in the Sadducees' encounter with Jesus, when their leader asked him the question about the woman with seven husbands — ending with the sixty-four-dollar question: "Whose wife will she be in the resurrection?" Jesus knew it was a trick question, because he knew the source. From the Sadducee point of view, what difference did it make, since the only significant thing about life was getting along here and now? Jesus' answer, "God is the God of the living not the dead," was his way of cutting through the false dilemma. While the here and now is the only stage upon which we really face decisions, we cannot solve our problems simply by ignoring the background. What we do is tested in the crucible of life, and the results are not theoretical but quite practical, in that everyone will sooner or later run into the practical results of his own previous choices.

The Sadducee always attempts to concentrate solely on the problem of death by being perfectly willing to accept and adjust to whatever comes. But life does not work out so simply. Man is not a chameleon — historically, intellectually, or religiously. He cannot understand life's demands solely with reference to his own self. The present is always alive, but it is never encountered without a past and future. Decisions involve judgments.

Yet the Sadducee answer to the problem of religion is rooted deeply in human nature, and can never be overcome by being exposed nor eliminated by argument. It is natural for us to attempt to solve our problems passively, and to hope that if we do not commit ourselves our problems will solve themselves. Furthermore, it is a plain fact that nobody can wrestle with every possible question that may arise. We do have to limit our commitments in daily living. The Sadducee is not only typical of one element in human nature which tries to solve life's problems with a half-solution. He also represents a good deal of common sense. There is no point in denying that.

The Pharisee is in direct contradiction to the Sadducee. He always attempts to eliminate the problem of death by concen-

trating solely on that of guilt. If man's allegiance to a formula, to a system, to a code of behavior, to a ritual method of solving his problems, is unswerving, no situation can possibly arise where he will not be armed by his constant convictions. Death is no longer a significant issue for those who have disposed of it by so complete a concern with an adequate reply to the question of guilt. In theory, man's conscience is at ease because he knows he has done all that is required of him; he has nothing to be afraid of in new situations.

In the New Testament, the Pharisees are not given so good a reputation as that to which they were historically entitled. They made Pharisaic Judaism the spiritual oasis of the ancient world. Wherever Jewish synagogues were found throughout the Roman Empire, there the Gentile community would know that men were among them who believed in living by moral convictions, and who would maintain those convictions to the death. Furthermore, the Gentile community could know, if it cared, that here were men who were not simply victims of anxiety, drifting along in a meaningless world from which the old gods had withdrawn. Here, instead, were men who had an affirmation to make, who believed that life could be made good by human effort and human loyalty.

The Pharisee approach to life is essentially optimistic. It believes that no question can arise that cannot be given an adequate moral solution and disposed of completely then and there. It believes that no decision can ever confront men who live by a high moral code that will be impossible to meet. The only problem to be overcome in building a perfect world is the terrific, yet soluble, problem of man's disloyalty to the best he knows.

The Pharisees, likewise, asked Jesus a trick question. When they showed him the tribute money and asked him whether it was legal to give tribute to Caesar, they were trying to embarrass him so that he would compromise or try to evade. If he did that, he was no longer a spiritual threat to them, because in their eyes he would be self-condemned. But Jesus understood that he was being tested on the adequacy of living by formula much more than he was on a current political question, and by his answer he showed them that the problem of death cannot simply be eliminated.

Whether or not the Pharisee liked it, Caesar was in control. Roman currency was in circulation. One could try to ignore the facts by concentrating on moral theory, if he chose, but he would be no less under the rule, protection, and judgment of Roman power. In other words, a religious answer that does not come to terms with the practical problems that frame men's lives, and that has no social relevance to the world in which they live, is incomplete, no matter how noble its ethic may sound.

The Sadducee answer to life's problems is to ignore as many of them as possible. The Pharisee answer to life's problems is to relate them to one single, simple solution, which is supposed to suffice for everything. As a matter of fact, the Sadducees were never completely consistent, because they would not compromise all the way where the Jewish law was concerned. That had to be maintained. And the Pharisees were not completely consistent, since as living men and women they had to make practical adjustments in order to keep going, and they did so.

Each represents a great truth. No religious answer can be practical that defies our common sense. Neither can any religious answer command our loyalty unless it has a real center beyond our immediate selves — a mission to the world. Each represents the error of half-truth. Simple pragmatism may often be sensible, but it leaves man at the mercy of whatever occurs and without guidance as to what to do. Moral idealism may often be inspiring, but it never applies itself to a complicated world of human affairs and mixed motives.

The religious history of the human race is that men do seek to live by one or both of these ways of dealing with their problems. As a result they are never completely able to handle the problems of death and guilt in a real world. The one ignored will not remain that way and reasserts itself destructively. The Pharisee and the Sadducee represent man's natural religious attitude at its very best, but also show man's natural failure.

Even with the one-sidedness of the Pharisee approach to the problem of religion, it does represent one significant advance over the point of view of the Sadducee. The Pharisee through his very understanding of the problem is prevented from thinking of it in other than universal terms. He cannot conceive of there being an adequate solution to the problem of guilt which does not in principal involve everyone. The historic Pharisee thought the destiny of Israel to be as the moral example of the whole world — war would be eliminated, poverty brought to an end, and exploitation of man by man banished from the face of the earth.

The vision of Isaiah is the best answer of the Pharisee understanding of the destiny of Israel: " The Spirit of the Lord God is upon me; because the Lord hath anointed me to preach good tidings unto the meek; he hath sent me to bind up the broken-hearted, to proclaim liberty to the captives, and the opening of the prison to them that are bound; to proclaim the acceptable year of the Lord, and the day of vengeance of our God; to comfort all that mourn." If the prophecy is understood literally or symbolically; or if it is understood to refer primarily to Israel — as it probably did — or immediately to the whole world, nevertheless, it is a description of a religious answer, which relates the individual's faith to a wider circle and offers its promise on the basis of the acceptance of a common faith.

In this sense of relating the religious answer of the individual or of the special group to the general religious need of mankind, the Pharisee approach to religion represents the highest attainment of man's sense of moral responsibility.

When the statement is made that a man cannot be a Christian until he has first been a Jew, this Pharisee sense of universal responsibility is the point in mind. Even though the Pharisee does not recognize the implications of the threat of death, yet he does know that common sense is not enough to live by, because its range of vision is too small. Until the religion of individuals and groups involves the acceptance of as wide ranges of concern as necessary, if sense is to be made of experience, their faith will never have asked the question that Christianity purports to answer.

CHAPTER V

The Great If

IF THE world were other than it is, there would perhaps be no need for religion. If all the aspects of human experience fitted together neatly and logically so that we could always tell where we are going and why, we should not have to act on faith. We could act with sight, and sight would be the only necessity for adequate living. The Epistle to the Hebrews is only being realistic when it says, " Faith is the substance of things hoped for, the evidence of things not seen." The kind of world we live in demands that we act on the basis of convictions, if we are going to act, without final guarantees.

The real power of the threats of death and guilt is in their combination of reality and unknowability. We know the threats to be real, but we cannot ever see our problem with such completeness as to be able to dispose of it permanently. Even where we act by a creative kind of faith, the next transition or the next decision raises the whole question of meaningfulness over again. If the world were other than it is, so that we could depend upon sight by itself, rather than upon insight, there would perhaps be no need for religion.

If the world were different in another way, the religious problem might exist, but perhaps it could be given a permanent solution. While we might have to continue living by faith, we could be assured that our faith was correct. To be sure, in this other kind of world we could never prove mathematically where we are going or why, but the value of faith would be demonstrated by results, so that once a man was willing to live by the particular insight involved, the problem of life would consist only of repeated applications.

The great difficulty with which all proposed religious solutions have to contend is that the threats of death and guilt continue. Even faith does not dispose of them forever. When a man acts by faith in an immediate decision, he goes on in spite of the threats, but they may very well continue to plague him about his decision, and they are sure to arise again in connection with his next one. In other words, it is impossible to conduct one's life in such a way that the decisive nature of decisions is eliminated. The only alternatives are accepting the problem of decision for what it is or else trying to evade it.

If the world were other than it is, the problem of bringing up children would be a simple process in principle, even though the many-sided nature of human life would make it still demanding as far as time and concentration are concerned. But the problem of bringing up children is essentially an experimental venture, in which what works well with one child may not work well with the next, and where adequate handling of the problem at one stage in the child's development is no guaranty of being able to handle it adequately at the next stage. The process of bringing up children turns out to be one of applying a living faith — an interpretation of parent-child relationships by which one is willing to live — to all sorts of situations, many of which cannot be foreseen at all and many which are sensed rather than fully appreciated.

If the world were other than it is, international relations would turn out to be primarily the process of applying known economic and social laws to situations, with the assurance that by either logic or faith, or both, the groups and blocs and races and nations that make up the population of the world would always act in terms of long-range self-interest. But men and women, both as individuals and groups, do not in practice act on the basis of what would appear to be objectively their self-interest. Men and women differ as to what is their self-interest. They differ as to what are the economic and social laws, and even as to whether there are really any such things.

If the world were other than it is, mankind could count on progress, and assume that basic lessons once learned would not have to be learned over again, either by individuals or groups. If this were the case, the world would treasure its achievements and retain the skills and techniques it had acquired until they were improved either technically or morally. If the world were other than it is, we should not have to worry about the possibilities for evil, which seem inevitably to be associated with every new possibility for good — for instance, atomic energy as the new prime mover for a new material standard of living, or as the destructive agent of civilization.

The fact is that the world is as it is. It is not some other way. Consequently, man's religious problem can never be "put on ice." It has to be faced in every new situation we encounter, and although we may certainly bear future probabilities in mind as we make our decisions today, we dispose only of details in the process. We never dispose of the problem of fundamental meaningfulness, which recurs again and again and again. We live in a world where man has no choice but to live by some kind of faith, and where he has to subject that faith — regardless of what claims may be made about it — to practical tests in every transition along life's way and in every significant decision that confronts him.

Under these circumstances, both the Sadducee and the Pharisee approaches to religion are continually on trial. Since these two approaches represent two sides of our own natures, even though we tend to emphasize one more than the other, this means that the real demands of a real world are always testing the faith by which we live, with our security, status, and achievement at stake. Our children's needs cannot be ignored even if we do not handle them intelligently. Our business or home activity, even when it appears to be one hundred per cent repetitive, by the very fact of continuance raises questions of meaningfulness in our minds. We may not be interested in politics and economics, but we cannot move out of a world in which political and economic developments influence our opportunities. All of us have to face the possibility or actuality of physical illness. All of us have to be able to do something about the deaths of those we love.

Since the world is not other than it is, and since these and many other questions that raise the threats of death and guilt cannot be disposed of in advance, religion becomes the process of dealing continually with the question of meaningfulness. And the only test possible for any religious approach is whether it enables men to find an adequate security, status, and achievement in a world which is accepted for what it is. If the nature of life is distorted and if its elements are ignored, there is always a possibility that the whole religious structure will be demolished by events.

It is human nature to want to be safe. It is natural to want results guaranteed in advance. Men are always trying to narrow the limits of the unpredictable and the uncertain, suggesting that somehow the term "faith" refers to the unreasonable, as in the expression "blind faith." But, properly understood, faith refers to the fact that the most important relationships in life are not susceptible of mathematical verification. You cannot measure love or loyalty by any formula, no matter how many variables you put into it — yet without some love and loyalty life is sterilized and untrue to itself.

However, since our need for safety and security is what it is, people are always trying to rephrase the universe in order to be assured that their faith works, even though they end by living in an artificial and false universe. The tragedy of Willie Loman in *The Death of a Salesman* lies in his need to be " successful" as the measure of the meaning of his life, while the relationships with his wife and sons, which might have given him real depth and power, are sacrificed at the altar of his false gods.

If the world were other than it is, men might be able to solve life's problems in the Sadducee way by adjustment. But the world is as it is, and the problem must be faced as to whether the Sadducee answer to the problem does not require men to live by self-deception. The Sadducee has to tell himself that he can be the practical center of his own universe, regardless of what theoretical external loyalties he may acknowledge. Can the Sadducee carry his faith out in practice? The history of the world and our own acquaintance with ourselves and those around us show that he can carry it out as long as he is allowed to ignore pressures over which he has no control.

The Sadducees of history tried to solve their problems by compromising with the Romans, but eventually the demands were more than could be met by a policy of adjustment. In other words, compromise may be necessary in practice, but as a theory of life it becomes a dilemma, which raises either such contradictions in circumstances as to make men helpless or such contradictions in their thinking as to paralyze action. When the Sadducees of Jerusalem were pushed to the extreme, they had to fight back and go down to death in the ruins of their own city. Man may eliminate the problem of guilt as a conscious concern, and concentrate only on the problem of death, but he eventually faces a situation where guilt reappears in the form of making him choose between the death of his autonomy or the death of meaningfulness.

When men and women try to live by adjustment to circumstance, they are continually forced to face the question as to whether life is worth living, whether they are really themselves, when they simply try to identify themselves with history. The question may not loom large in consciousness until difficult circumstances make it, but it remains as an underlying note of anxiety in the heart of the most consistent Sadducee. When a family that has tried to solve life's meaning through the most irresponsible type of country club life loses its money, it has to choose between continuing the pattern of irresponsibility and beginning over again. When a Christian Scientist, whose creed is one of the more respectable forms of Sadduceeism, encounters cancer in a loved one, he has to choose between ignoring reality and letting that loved one suffer senselessly or abandoning the evasion of reality in his own heart.

If the world were other than it is, the Sadducee approach to life might be practical. As things happen to be, the Sadducee serves to remind us of the necessity for common sense and compromise in many affairs, and also of the impossibility of making this attitude the cornerstone of life. As a matter of fact, the Sadducee temperament is so congenial to all of us in some moods, and to some of us most of the time, that it cannot be shaken except by the most serious questions, and then the result may be, not an acceptance of the challenge, but bitter resistance.

While the Sadducee, in trying to make life other than it is, concentrates on human weakness and tries to discount the pressure of events, the Pharisee concentrates on human strength and emphasizes the significance of events. But the Pharisee, likewise, has to rephrase the actualities of the world.

If men were other than they are, they might not build a perfect world, but they certainly would make the situation a lot better than it is now. The Pharisee has no doubt about the capacity of man to be consistently loyal to such a goal. The

Pharisee type may serve a number of different ideas of how a perfect world would appear, but all Pharisees are sure that if men are concerned enough they can make their lives meaningful, and also fulfill the destiny of mankind.

If the world ever needed an ethical ideal for its salvation, the books of the Prophets in the Old Testament supplied it. The proclamation in Isaiah of what would happen if Israel were sufficiently loyal has an appeal to reality. This would, indeed, be a much better world, if not an entirely perfect one, if all men tried to live consistently by their noblest moral insights. The problem is not in the vision of the Jewish law, but in the historic understanding by the Pharisees, who accepted it as how human nature works. In spite of the appeal of the prophets, Israel never provided the example in its fullness. In spite of the theory of the " remnant " — that a small loyal minority could serve instead of the whole of Israel — the example was never supplied sufficiently. Abraham's argument with God about the number of righteous men necessary to make it worth God's while to save Sodom and Gomorrah from destruction is a parable of the problem. The number is continually reduced, but eventually Sodom and Gomorrah are destroyed. Man may eliminate the problem of death as a conscious concern, and concentrate only on that of guilt, but the pressure of circumstances, particularly those arising from the drives of human nature, will eventually force him, even though he may not recognize it, into a place where the moral choice is meaningless unless he is willing to have his religious formula die. Historically, Pharisaism has always begun as a practical reform movement emphasizing a high moral discipline against a decadent social climate. And historically, Pharisaism has always run into situations in which the formula no longer fits, and the moral choice was not so much one of loyalty to the formula as one of whether to retain it or not. The Protestant Reformation is an excellent example of this. The Pharisaic theory of Western Catholicism in the sixteenth century was meaningless in its social application and in its understanding of man and history under the circumstances of the new developments of civilization. The Protestant moral choice was to reject the Western Catholic formula in order to apply more fundamental Christianity to a real world's real problems. The alternative loyalty would have led to the irrelevance of Christianity as a whole. The Counter-Reformation movement a half century later, which changed what was left of the medieval Church in radical ways, proved the Reformation premises to have been right, even though differing with the conclusions.

Our modern world is now wrestling with the problem of whether its political and economic traditions really fit the needs of modern society. The Manchester school of economics, the prevailing theory of the last half of the nineteenth century in England and in the United States, held that ever-expanding production in a truly competitive system would, by the automatic working out of economic law, provide a good life for everyone. The moral choice appears to be whether we are willing to die to this tradition of political economy, which has for many people been their religion as well as their social life, in order to build a world in which the realities of human nature and the realities of a technical age may be brought into functional relationship. Loyalty to what worked in the nineteenth century may well make the whole of Western civilization irrelevant in these days of the atomic bomb.

An interesting parallel to the same problem of Pharisaic loyalty is given in Marxist circles, where the real moral question now appears to be: In what way may the genuine and lasting insights of the nineteenth century socialist analysis be made available for the building of a democratic world today? Loyalty to the Marxist tradition, as such, forces its adherents into a choice between two different kinds of meaninglessness — that of Communism, which destroys the human values systematically and makes the old goal unattainable, and that of the traditional Social Democrat, who often is unable to make intelligent political choices and to take adequate political action, no matter how orthodox his theories may be.

The Pharisee approach to religion runs head on into the problem of human nature in relationship to the world. The Pharisee approach to religion is unable to see that the very process of having a formula is in itself dangerous. If man accepts a formula, he may deceive himself about its applicability and about his own performance. If he rejects it, his religious problem is given an unreal cast so that it is difficult to deal with it. The conflict between the Roman Catholic Church and Communism, for instance, is between two different forms of Pharisaism, where, in each case, those who are loyal brand their enemies as being against religion as they understand it. Although Communists may not use the term " religion," their propaganda shows that religion is what they mean.

Even if there were no problem of the details of particular formulas becoming obsolete in a changing world, the Pharisee approach to religion has the more basic problem of man's loyalty to deal with. When men acknowledge the claims of loyalty upon them, no problem has been solved. It has just been translated into somewhat different terms with a new factor added. Men may either assume their pledged loyalty to be more meaningful than it is when it comes to making sense out of life or they may assume their performance to be much better than it is. In either case, the man who has tried to solve his religious questions by loyalty to a formula tends to blind himself to new problems growing out of the formula, since his appreciation of the dynamic structure of human nature is inadequate. The Marxist cannot see very easily the fact that Communism has its own corruption in its use of power. The Roman Catholic Church does not understand that the institution that is not open to criticism by its members can never be flexible enough to be the basis for the real solution of their real problems, but can serve their needs only by distorting their human nature.

The Pharisee approach, in the last analysis, suffers from its tendency to oversimplify the cause for man's religious problem. The human situation must include functional relationships as well as discriminations of ethical value. It must include distinctions of taste and meaning as well as economic issues. When the situation is oversimplified, men are neither able to appreciate the realities of history nor to understand the unsolved and unfaced problems which threaten their security, status, and achievement. By accepting a formula purporting to handle the problems of guilt and thus make life meaningful, men may be left that much more unprepared to deal with the unavoidable threat of death.

There is no example of the Pharisee approach to life's meaning that does not spring out of the real recognition of a real need, no matter how it may oversimplify the issue and no matter how many other problems it may avoid. This world can, indeed, be made a lot more pleasant to live in, a lot more just to the vast majority of its inhabitants, and a lot less dangerous for all by the resolute attack on specific problems and by the loyalty of men and women to movements designed to attain specific objectives. If life were other than it is, if the world were other than it is, the Pharisee approach to religion would achieve inward peace, regardless of what else it accomplished. But since the world is as it is, the great IF remains.

In the last anaylsis, a monotheism that does not bring its adherents to their knees, not only in a real recognition of a real demand of universal proportions but also in penitent acknowledgment of their own part in the difficulties in the way of mankind, cannot be an adequate faith for all circumstances. Actually, before the great IF can be disposed of, man needs not only penitence — a frank recognition of his plight — but also redemption, which is the ability to do something about it. The polytheist does not see the problem this way. Both the Sadducee and the Pharisee recognize the issue, with the former hoping to bypass it and the later hoping to overcome it by a frontal attack. The history of the world and the perplexity of our age are demonstrations that the great IF remains, and that man is still uncertain as to how to find the faith that will meet life's tests.

If an ideal moral solution to the religious problems of the world had been possible, Pharisaic Judaism would have supplied the need. Its range was universal at best, and its understanding of the meaning of the worship of one God was basically realistic. And it did point to meaningful answers to the specific difficulties in man's personal conduct and social life, which threatened his security, status, and achievement and raised the basic threats of guilt and death. The application of Pharisee religion to life was in terms of a high personal and social ethic, which had the advantage over some other ethical statements in that its meaning directly related man to his group, and did not leave him in the illusion of individual and moral superiority. Nevertheless, Pharisee religion, in its Jewish form, and in the derivative and parallel forms which have developed since, has never been fulfilled sufficiently to stabilize the meaning of life for men, to say nothing of stabilizing the world. There is no formula that by itself can solve the problem, regardless of the magnitude of its conception of God and the nobility of its ideal of worship.

Men must be able to deal functionally with the threats of guilt and death arising from the transitions they go through, the decisions they are forced to make, and the external pressures that influence their thought and action, if life is to be essentially meaningful. The Pharisee and Sadducee are types of the perennial human reaction to this problem, but while each contains an element of truth, and while the Pharisee response at its best re-lates the individual man to the whole human race, nevertheless, neither provides an adequate basis for meeting the problem. The threats of death and guilt still remain. They cannot be ignored. They must be met somehow. The religious history of mankind is the story of the search for the way by which they may be met.

If human nature were other than it is, there would be no prob-lem, but since it is as it is, the problem has to be dealt with.

CHAPTER VI

The Cross

CHRISTIAN faith asserts that there is an adequate answer to the problem of religion which will meet all the tests of history, of human nature, and of the fundamental threats encountered in living. Christian faith asserts that living people may become new persons here and now, so that they will see their lives in a new way, and their relationships to their problems will be on a new basis. Christian faith points to Jesus as the Christ because men and women who have contact with him find this to be the only real and creative answer to the problems of death and guilt — an answer that does not require them to ignore part of life's evidence, nor to falsify the nature of the problem in whole or in part. Christian faith accords honor to Jesus because of the reorientation of life which men and women have found and continue to find for themselves through contact with him.

Paul was not just speculating about Jesus when he wrote in the Epistle to the Philippians: " Wherefore God hath highly exalted him, and given him a name which is above every name: that at the name of Jesus every knee shall bow, of things in heaven, and things in earth, and things under the earth; and that every tongue should confess that Jesus Christ is Lord, to the glory of God the Father." Paul was interpreting his own experience in such a way that others might be able to use it in solving their own religious problems. He had prefaced this paean by saying, " Let this mind be in *you*, which was also in Christ Jesus: who being in the form of God, thought it not robbery to be equal with God: but made himself of no reputation, and took upon him the form of a servant, and was made in the likeness of men: and being found in fashion as a man, he humbled himself, and became obedient unto death, even the death of the cross."

The Peter who is reported in the book of The Acts as asserting about Jesus, "Therefore let all the house of Israel know assuredly, that God hath made that same Jesus, whom ye have crucified, both Lord and Christ," was reflecting his own personal experience as a transformed personality. Men are really transformed only when they discover what appears to be a fully satisfying and meaningful answer to the problem of religion for their own personal lives. Such a transformation has seemed, indeed, to have occurred in the lives of many people without having any lasting significance. It can be real, creative, and vital only when it is not merely an emotional reaction but a realistic interpretation of the meaning of experience which enables those who discover it to appreciate an adequate security, status, and achievement in their own lives while in the midst of real problems of the real world.

Men and women can find the Christian faith to be their own religion in any vital sense only if they share in some real way the experience of Paul and Peter. It does not mean that they phrase life's meaning in New Testament terminology. It does mean that they, like Paul and Peter, feel convinced that contact with Jesus has enabled them to find the realistic way to handle the problems of guilt and death. Men and women are only theoretically interested, if at all, in speculative opinions about the Bible, about Jesus, about creeds and customs of the churches. They are directly interested in answers to the problems of guilt and death, because the need for an adequate security, status, and achievement is not something that can be ignored. To the extent that men and women feel and see the connection between the New Testament proclamations about Jesus and their problems as real men in a real world, to that extent Christianity is not just an awareness that the traditional institutions of the Christian religion (in an organized sense) have had and still have a pervasive, environmental influence from which none of us is completely separated. Rather, Christianity is the source of life and the power of life for men and women who feel and know that the gospel answers the questions they are really asking.

When the members of a so-called Christian culture read in the first chapter of John's Gospel: "For the law was given by Moses, but grace and truth came by Jesus Christ. No man hath seen God at any time; the only begotten Son, which is in the bosom of the Father, he hath declared *him*," they are only reading statements made about a stranger. To be sure, they have heard somewhat of this stranger, and they cannot avoid the indirect marks of his influence. But the statement is not necessarily speaking to them about their God. It may be just words. If, however, the people who read these verses have found Jesus Christ to be the means through which they are able to deal adequately with the pressures of guilt and death, then these statements are luminous. Certainly, men have known the meaning of moral obligation and what obedience might accomplish. Jesus was not needed to bring us this lesson. But "grace and truth" are other matters. The desire to fulfill the law from the heart, the feeling of being at one with the purpose of the universe, the freedom from guilt and death, which one knows is not illusory, the sense of belonging to a fellowship that bridges the divisions between men — these are "grace and truth," and they matter immensely. It is no wonder that the response of Christian faith is that apart from Jesus Christ we have had only the foggiest notion of what it meant to be related creatively to life's overruling and central demand. We have a new basis of relationship to the world, to our own psychological and physio-logical needs, to the communities in which we are placed, and to the historical forces which frame our lives. It is no wonder that we say, if we know the Christian gospel in our hearts, " No man hath seen God at any time; the only begotten Son, which is in the bosom of the Father, he hath declared *him*."

The Christian gospel is not a series of claims about the rela-tionship of Jesus, a man who lived in Palestine two thousand years ago, to the main currents of the universe, except through the faith of those who hear the proclamation. In terms of ab-stract, objective theory, the claims mean nothing. It is not so much a matter of their theoretical truth or falsity as it is a matter of their irrelevance to those who are not moved to live and think and act on their basis. The real problem for men and women is that of coming to terms with the facts of guilt and death. The Christian gospel asserts that those who know Jesus as their Christ can do so. The next question is, How can these claims be understood so that they are the real answers to the real questions we are asking?

The Pharisee sought to approach the problem of religion by concentrating on the issue of guilt and ignoring that of death. If he was loyal, eventualities would take care of themselves, and he was confident of the overruling love of God. That is what the Pharisee faith in the resurrection, as a hope, meant. The man who is completely loyal can meet what comes — if he is completely loyal. The Pharisee also thought of the destiny of the loyal man as providing the moral example needed by the whole world. First, he had thought of Israel as a whole, but then, more realistically, of a smaller loyal remnant instead of the whole na-tion. In Christian faith Jesus becomes the saving remnant, and fulfills completely the demands of loyalty by dying on a cross. This both fulfills and contradicts Pharisee theory, because the result looks like a defeat instead of victory. The cross has always worried men and women who think that the value and meaning of life have to be measured in terms of some kind of objective accomplishment as the reward for loyalty — perhaps a reward which others use instead of ourselves, because the world has always been able to understand heroes and martyrs, but still an accomplishment. The fulfillment of the demand of loyalty can be made available in the case of Jesus, however, only to those who share his faith.

The Sadducee sought to approach the problem of religion by concentrating on the problem of death and ignoring that of guilt, but the purpose was to make life's immediacy satisfying even if the total picture remained incomprehensible. That is why the Sadducee denied the resurrection — as a hope — since he could find no sense to experience as a whole, only to that part which he controlled for the moment in some manner. Jesus with the cross both fulfilled and contradicted the Sadducee theory. Here was as complete an example of adjustment to circumstance as the world has ever known, but it did not result in a sense of mastery in any way at all. It concluded with the act of dying, and dying in such a way that the whole event was objectively frustrating and meaningless. It was exactly what Sadducee political policy was designed to avoid. The fulfillment of the demand of adjustment to the reality of circumstance, in the case of Jesus, can be understood and shared only by those who share the faith of Jesus.

The cross, historically, began with a direct and open challenge by Jesus to the pretensions of both Pharisees and Sadducees — a challenge which could not be ignored. It was no gesture in the way of heroics, but the logical conclusion to the kind of faith by which Jesus lived, as well as the ultimate demonstration of its meaningfulness in the context of the real situation. Jesus lived his faith. He did not just talk about it. The challenge was part of that living.

The cross began, in its final chapter, with the cleansing of the Temple. It had begun potentially, of course, with the beginning of Jesus' ministry. The Temple, objectively speaking, needed cleansing. It was corrupt in practice. It was irrelevant in much of its detail. Yet it was the center and symbol of the Jewish national life, and as such represented — particularly to the Sadducee, yet psychologically to the Pharisee as well — a security, status, and achievement basis which was comforting. To criticize the Temple was to criticize the way men understand life's meaning and, consequently, to threaten their security, status, and achievement. With the Sadducee the criticism was direct and overt because the administration of the Temple was the Sadducee privilege — a privilege permitted them by the Romans as the reward for their compromise. With the Pharisee, the threat was indirect but just as real, because it required subjecting their theory of loyalty to questioning. Jesus did not threaten so much the basis of their security, status, and achievement, in the Temple itself, as he threatened it in their understanding of loyalty. He had no authority to do the cleansing and, although it may have been needed, it was a dangerous act.

The result of Jesus' act was to make direct the condemnation implicit in the two trick questions — of the woman with the seven husbands and the tribute money (see Chapter IV, pp. 64 f.). Jesus was arrested and condemned. He was sentenced by Pilate and taken out and executed. Thus far the cross is only an example of what Jesus himself did to handle his own problems of guilt and death, which were his in the same way in which they confront any living human being. The connection of the cross with our lives would be very indirect if that was all there was to it. But the cross is not only an example; it is a direct application of vital religion to the heart of any person who appreciates his own connection with it.

Down through the years the Christian Church has used seven

statements, which were said to have been made by Jesus on the cross, as texts for special meditation about the significance of the event. Whether or not they were his actual words is unimportant. But they do focus Christian faith precisely and accurately, and they are true to what we understand of Jesus. In a sense, they make him our Christ, since we understand his significance for us and for our ability to deal with the problems of guilt and death, as we behold him interpreted by these statements. In our understanding here we need deal only with the first, fourth, and seventh, although the others can also be used for the purpose of illuminating the religious question and answer.

In the first statement of the cross, Jesus said, "Father, forgive them; for they know not what they do." Here is an example of magnanimity. Here is an example of how the man of sensitivity and insight deprives the most painful experience of its full bitterness. He refuses to be on the defensive against it. He recognizes the confusion of understanding on the part of those responsible. But this statement by itself would never make Jesus anyone's Christ. At best he would be just a good example of the spirit by which suffering is borne best, particularly suffering caused by the action of other people. This statement makes Jesus a magnanimous martyr, but there have been many others who have done likewise in parallel circumstances — Socrates drinking the hemlock, Stephen facing the stones. Nobility inspires us to emulate it should we also be victims, but it also depicts a kind of superiority over us, because we all know all too well that we do not easily or naturally rise to this kind of height of understanding.

With the fourth word from the cross, however, the contact between those who are seeking for an adequate religious statement for their lives and Jesus Christ is made clear and explicit. Here the problem of guilt is met and faced for what it is. And it is met in such a way that we too can identify ourselves with the question and answer. As a matter of fact, Christian people have been doing this all through the ages. In the fourth word from the cross, Jesus becomes our Christ.

"My God, my God, why hast thou forsaken me?" These words have often been treated as a cry of despair, but their meaning is more profound. Actually they are part of the first line of Psalm 22: "My God, my God, look upon me; why hast thou forsaken me? and art so far from my health, and from the words of my complaint?" Psalm 22 is a Day of Atonement psalm, a sort of "General Confession" of the Jewish Church. The speaker is never simply the solitary individual, but rather the whole house of Israel, and the individual speaker of the words is identifying himself with the house of Israel by mean of a liturgical act. The nature of this identification is most important, because it is an admission of individual and group sin. The speaker identifies himself with the sin of Israel, admitting himself to be a participant.

It was the genius of Jewish religion to make progressively more profound discoveries of the moral meaning of history. Man's distress is at least partly the result of man's own moral failure, and while there may be exceptions to the rule on the individual level, it is an accurate description of man's social life. But, it was also the genius of the Old Testament religion to realize that the individual could never be cut off religiously from his society. He was the bearer of its destiny — he was its potential redeemer and he also shared in its burden of failure. The old Rabbinic proverb, "If one Jew were to keep the whole law for twenty-four hours, then Israel would be restored," is an illustration of the point. On the Day of Atonement, each Jew has always felt himself partly responsible for the suffering of Israel, and has taken upon himself the blame for its sorrow.

Jesus on the cross refused to separate himself in moral superiority from the house of Israel, from which he had come. He refused to assert a moral superiority against his world. Instead, he identified himself with the Israel of history, repeating the Day of Atonement psalm. By this means, Jesus realistically met the problem of guilt in its most extreme form. He refused to try to justify himself, when every normal human tendency would point in that direction. Instead, he, who was a victim of man's failure to face up to the problem of guilt, admitted his share in the same problem. He identified himself with Israel, and hence with all mankind, since Israel is the symbol of mankind seeking real solutions to real problems. Here is nothing morbid. Here is no gesture. The fact was true. Jesus was of Israel historically, and his confession made sense. But it signified that complete abandonment of complacency and self-righteousness at the inner core of being which alone can make it possible to deal with the problem of guilt completely.

Jesus identified himself with those who crucified him, and hence with all those who, like the people of Jerusalem, try to save themselves by crucifying others. Jesus, on the cross, identified himself with us, if we understand ourselves and our own motivations honestly enough to recognize the identity of ourselves with the Pharisees and Sadducees of long ago. As Jesus, on the cross, identifies himself with us, so we can make in return the same identification, and meet the problem of guilt on the same level that he did.

The fourth word from the cross means practically that the men and women who understand its relevance to themselves and to their world are given a new relationship to the problems that concern them. To take Jesus as one's Christ means to recognize that we can deal more adequately with the obstinacy of our own children, the apathy of our communities to real issues, the lack of co-operation of our business associates, the obtuseness of our friends when we are trying to arouse their interest, and, above all, with our own frustrations once we accept the reality of guilt as Jesus did. We complicate our actions and confuse our understandings when we have to defend ourselves from ourselves and from our neighbors and partners and even our enemies, at the same time that we try to act in living situations. The man who faces the problem of guilt realistically, saying, "These are the facts; now where do we go from here?" is able to face situations with a new objectivity. As an honest man, he knows he can never be perfect himself, nor can he expect perfection from others. But he can do the best he can with what he has under the circumstances, without feeling on the defensive against life, provided he is honest with himself about his connections with the problems that concern him.

The seventh word from the cross also comes from The Psalms. Jesus is said to have concluded the ordeal of the cross by crying out, "Father, into thy hands I commend my spirit." This is another liturgical use — this time one of dedication rather than penitence. The phrase comes from Psalm 31 — "Into thine hand I commit my spirit: thou hast redeemed me, O Lord God of truth." It is an expression of the corporate faith of Israel that, although immediate circumstances were difficult, nevertheless, the promises of God would be fulfilled if Israel remained faithful.

The Day of Dedication in Israel was the anniversary of the reconsecration of the Temple after the Maccabean wars. The Temple had been defiled by the soldiers of Antiochus Epiphanes, the Greek-Syrian emperor, who had tried to unify his dominions by turning everybody into "Greeks" with Greek customs, Greek education, and Greek religious practice. But some of the Jews had refused to conform and had been martyred in the first religious persecution in history. They had died for what they believed to be right without having any way of knowing that their cause would ever win out in a practical, historical way. How could Jewish guerrillas defeat the Macedonian phalanx? When the historical fluke happened, and Judas Maccabeus and John Hyrcanus restored the Jewish kingdom so that the Temple could be reconsecrated, people could not help remembering the loyalty and faith of the Antiochian martyrs. The predominant note is: We will trust God's providence regardless of what happens to us. It is the same note as that of Jesus' prayer in the Garden of Gethsemane, " Father, . . . not my will, but thine, be done."

In the use of this liturgical verse, Jesus came to terms with the problem of death in such a way that those who are identified with him, through their faith, are enabled to make the same kind of commitment themselves. The outcome of human problems cannot always be foreseen. Sometimes technical difficulties are long-range problems, and sometimes they are insoluble problems, but the man of the Christian faith can go ahead.

In using these words from The Psalms, Jesus accepted the reality of physical death as a natural phenomenon. The only realistic way to face the unknown future is to do the best one can now and go ahead trusting God for what happens. Life is not so constructed that guarantees can be found in advance. The man who waits until all the evidence is in before acting will never act, whether he is considering his own marriage or trying to make a political decision.

The cross was a full recognition of the reality of both guilt and death, each with the other. Jesus' recognition of the problem of guilt was made in full acceptance of the other half of man's religious difficulty; and Jesus' acceptance of the problem of death was made without self-righteousness. Neither vindication nor assurance, nor self-satisfaction, mars Jesus' affirmation of life's meaning — identification with mankind and confidence in over-reaching divine purpose which he might serve, even though he could see no personal escape from his historical situation. This is no blank resignation, but rather a positive affirmation of the possibilities for meaningful living which can be discovered in any and every situation. Here is no denial of the brute facts which so often make our lives hard but, on the contrary, here is a relationship to life's practical problems in which the complicating, confusing forces of guilt and death are dealt with, leaving man free to face technical problems without being poisoned in advance.

To speak of the cross of Christ, therefore, means the cross of "my Christ." The significance of the cross consists of the fact that Jesus' experience connects dynamically with my life. His experience becomes the lens through which we look at our problems, our responsibilities, and our opportunities. The cross is the gateway from one level of life to another, not just for Jesus, but for all who name themselves Christians. And the new level of life refers not to what may happen to us when we die, but to something that is real and immediate here and now. As Paul said, "I live; yet not I, but Christ liveth in me: and the life which I now live in the flesh I live by the faith of the Son of God, who loved me, and gave himself for me."

The standard visible Christian symbol is the cross. We find it on altars and steeples and carved in the wood of pulpits and pew ends. It is stamped in gilt on hymnbooks and prayer books. It is worn as costume jewelry. Perhaps the meaning of the cross, as understood in Christian faith, for our own lives — in terms of our participation in the experience of Jesus — can be clarified by thinking of these visible signs in this way:

When I look at a cross, I imagine that the crossarms are not there. I see only the upright. And what I see then is a capital "I." Here is the symbol of my own problem and the problem of my world. Here is the visible sign of my egotism and the collective egotism of economic and social groups, of races and nations. Here is the root cause of anxiety and misery in every situation everywhere down through all the ages of human history.

Here is the key to the question as to why my job is so often a frustration rather than a fulfillment. Here is the clue to why my family is marked so often by tense rivalries rather than by glad harmony. Here is the indication as to why the struggles between management and labor seem to move from the achievement of agreements to new problems which have greater meaning than simply difference of opinion as to working conditions, wages, and hours. Here is a parable of the international hostility which has dogged the United Nations ever since the signing of the San Francisco agreement. I, individually and collectively, am the weakest link in the chain of circumstance. I am the problem in the picture. When I look at the cross seriously, I have to look at myself and see myself in my self-concern and its tragic consequences.

Then the crossbar is replaced, and I see the "I" canceled. It is not annulled. It is not suppressed. This is not the denial of individuality. This is not the forcing of persons into a common mold in which the "I" has no meaning at all. There is nothing totalitarian about the cross of Christ. As I recognize myself in the "I" without the crossarms, so now I can see what it means to be a "We." But without the cancellation of the "I" in this sense of the crucifixion of my own egotism there can be no "We."

But I am the problem to start with. Merely to make the recognition intellectually solves nothing. It may even add to our difficulties, by accentuating the note of guilt without offering a living way out. The cross by itself may describe our problem and what the ideal answer ought to be. But as Christians we do not see the cross by itself. It is the gift of God. It is the earnest of the love of God in every situation in which we find ourselves.

The scandal of Christianity consists partly in the fact that the one thing we do not wish to give up is the unconditioned "I," yet the only serious rival there is to the Lordship of Almighty God is this "I" which is always tempted to usurp the role of God —

in our homes, our community relations, our business life, and in national and international affairs. The cross, then, is the only way of dealing with the problem, but only a cross that is the gift of God can ever deal with it. By ourselves we can only recognize intellectually the appropriateness of the answer — if, indeed, we can go that far. The power of a loving God makes it possible for us first to face and then to deal with the root problem of existence — the one that all of us will pass by if we can.

When we see the meaning of the cross in this light, we shall then see that it is never simply a once-and-for-all experience for us. It is a continual problem. Every new challenge I face, every new decision I am called upon to make, every response evoked from me by the demands of other people, all these raise the question as to whether the "I" remains paramount, usurping the throne of God, or whether the "I" is canceled by the love of the God and Father of our Lord Jesus Christ.

CHAPTER VII

The Resurrection

IN THE New Testament, the resurrection is the primary reality. The disciples in becoming apostles called themselves witnesses of the resurrection of Jesus Christ. The resurrection provided the cutting edge of their proclamation. Regardless of the different interpretations and descriptions of what may have happened in detail, the central fact stands out sharp and clear: there is a new life here and now, and anybody for whom Jesus Christ is Lord can share in it. This new life is as different from the ordinary tone of the world as day is from night, as light is from darkness.

Whatever we read about the resurrection in the New Testament, the most luminous fact of all is what happened to the men and women who were convinced of its reality. They were changed people, whose relationships to God, to each other, and to the world in general were completely revolutionized. The picture of the risen Jesus Christ is rather indistinct by itself. The real picture in strong color and vivid line is seen in the radiant and vibrant personalities of those who are associated with their risen Lord.

If the resurrection were merely the record in the Bible of what people a long time ago said about what happened to other people as the result of the return to history of a character from whom we are even more distantly removed, it could not have much convincing power today. But the resurrection is the story of changed lives, brought closer to God through Christ, brought closer to each other through Christ, dedicated to the healing of the world through Christ. This is as true of our day as it was of the first century.

The risen Lord took hold of the life of a Peter, who had blown hot and cold, and made him steady as "the rock." Within a few weeks after the public execution of a political criminal — for that is the way the indictment against Jesus was meant to be read — a Peter, who had denied ever knowing him, stood in the public square of Jerusalem and boldly proclaimed, "This Jesus, whom you have crucified, God hath made him both Lord and Christ." Such a proclamation could not be made without bringing a counterindictment against the police and the judiciary of Jerusalem, and policemen and judges do not like to be treated this way. The risen Lord, however, had changed Peter.

The risen Lord also took hold of a young British physician named Wilfred Grenfell in our day and sent him far from Harley Street to become the apostle of the fishing colonies of Newfoundland and Labrador. The risen Lord took hold of a respectable second-generation Indian Christian, V. H. Azariah, Y.M.C.A. Secretary in Madras, and made him the great missionary to the "untouchables" and the first great Christian statesman of the younger churches of the Orient. The risen Lord took hold of a gifted young German musician and physician and sent him to a task of witness-bearing at Lambarene in Central Africa, and the echoes have come from the jungle to the farthest corners of the modern world.

The risen Lord through modern apostles, whose contact was just as real and essentially the same as that of the first century, touched lives in the most out of the way places. The lives of many American servicemen were saved in the Solomon Islands by natives who risked their own to do so; and behind their acts was the work of John Coleridge Patteson, first missionary bishop of Melanesia, whose death as a martyr on the beach of Guadalcanal provided as effective a witness to that part of the world as the heroic deaths of the first and second generation apostles did in theirs.

The fact of the resurrection is attested by the changed lives of those for whom Jesus Christ is the Lord, but behind every changed life is a share in the cross. The change is never simply an improvement in character, even though that would be a by-product of it. Its real manifestation is found in that these lives now become living proclamations of the love and mercy of God. These are now lives that are given to telling the story of God's "mighty acts" by their concern as well as by their words.

Those who share in the resurrection at first hand wear no halos. They are not immune to failure. They know even more poignantly than they ever did before that all men are continually tempted by experience to play God. But, trusting in the Lord Christ, they can continue to make this recognition first of themselves and then of the groups in which they have a part and then of the larger circles of human relationships. Paul said, "The sting of death is sin." Our refusal to meet the problems of guilt and death for what they really are confuses every situation in which we are involved — because the refusal is never simply an intellectual dodging of questions but even more a practical evasion of responsibility. Only the Lord God of heaven and earth, the ruler of history, is related to circumstance in such a way that neither past nor future raises any threats. We are never so related to events, and we never shall be. The resurrection faith consists first of all of knowing this about ourselves, and then continuing to live gladly and gloriously in this world of problems sustained by the presence of the living Christ here and now.

Only a powerful resurrection faith could enable Paul to associate honestly the twin recognitions of the seventh chapter of Romans: (1) "For the good that I would, I do not: but the evil which I would not do, that I do. Now if I do that I would not, it is no more I that do it, but sin that dwelleth in me. . . . O wretched man that I am! who shall deliver me from the body of this death?" And in the next verse comes the answer: (2) "I thank God through Jesus Christ our Lord. . . . There is therefore now no condemnation to them which are in Christ Jesus, who walk not after the flesh, but after the Spirit."

Behind the New Testament description of what happened at the first Easter was a Jewish setting which colored it with rich associations of tradition and practice. While this is foreign to the experience of twentieth century America, perhaps a look at this background may explain how certain symbols came to be used, and make possible our effective appropriation of the same symbols for our own religious lives. To understand the connection between Jewish history and the first century Pharisaic understanding of the Passover, however, will not in itself make us share powerfully in the resurrection. But it can help us to be aware of its tremendous implications in a way that might otherwise escape us.

Participation in the resurrection here and now, however, is the central issue. Paul's proclamation to the Colossians said, "If ye then be risen with Christ, seek those things which are above." He was writing to the living members of the little congregation at Colossae, apparently expecting them to connect the resurrection with their everyday experience right then. And this means — as it meant for them — daring to face the realities of death and guilt in our experience, trusting God's sustaining love here and now, rather than depending upon our own virtue, our own intelligence, our own advantages, or upon anything else that is ours. Participating in the resurrection means for us that we continually ask help to meet our problems of home, community, business, and larger affairs in the light of the cross and that we count on receiving the help we ask for because we believe it is immediately available now and always. The risen Christ is with us as his cross becomes ours and his resurrection ours too.

The significance of this is brought out, perhaps, by remembering the Jewish Passover tradition. Jesus was arrested on the eve of the Passover, when every Jewish family was preparing the Passover meal, to be served at sundown the next day. Jesus was crucified on the day that would end with the lighting of the Passover candles and the beginning of the solemn festival. It is no wonder, then, that those close to Jesus associated his death with the Passover tradition, and that Christian tradition has borrowed the word "paschal" from Judaism, and speaks of Jesus as the Paschal victim. "Paschal" is an adjective derived from the Passover.

The Passover is the festival that commemorates the delivery of the Hebrew people from captivity in Egypt. The story, as told in the book of Exodus, and as repeated in every Jewish family on the observance of every Passover, begins with the marking of the doorposts of every Hebrew home with blood from a freshly killed lamb, followed by the escape of the people under the leadership of Moses, the successful crossing of the Red Sea, and finally the establishment of a covenant between God and Israel at Mount Sinai. In other words, the Passover is a picture of God's mercy and man's consequent obligation and responsibility.

The association of Easter with the Passover is borne out by the ancient hymn of Saint John of Damascus, coming down to us from the eighth century, and found in the hymnals of many denominations today:

> "Come, ye faithful, raise the strain
>   Of triumphant gladness!
>   God hath brought his Israel
>   Into joy from sadness,

> Loosed from Pharaoh's bitter yoke
> Jacob's sons and daughters,
> Led them with unmoistened foot
> Through the Red Sea waters."

Christ leads us through the problems of death and guilt (we associate them together in this discussion and refuse to think of one without the other lest its deeper spiritual meaning be destroyed) in a way parallel to that by which Moses led the Hebrew people from Egypt. Just as Moses led his people from physical slavery in Egypt — privation, misery, disease, and meaningless work — so Christ leads us through a frank facing of the key problems of experience, so that death and guilt no longer defeat us. This fact is the cornerstone of Christian confidence.

In the ancient Passover story the Hebrew people were delivered from Egypt only after Moses had threatened an uncooperative Pharaoh a good many times; then finally came the threat of the destroying angel. If Pharaoh would not release the Hebrew people, then the angel would slay the first-born male in every Egyptian household. Every Hebrew family was told to kill an unblemished lamb and to mark the doorposts of its home with lamb's blood, so that the destroying angel would be able to distinguish between Hebrew and Egyptian homes. In every unmarked house the angel killed the first-born of every species, human and animal, and as a result the Egyptians were glad, for the moment, to have the Hebrews leave.

Since the Hebrews were actually saved, first from the destroying angel and then from the Egyptians, by the lamb's blood, it was natural for Christians to associate the death of Jesus on the cross with the killing of the lambs. But the association was more than one of coinciding dates — Good Friday and the Passover. The Hebrews were actually saved from physical bondage. Christians know themselves to be rescued from slavery to their lower selves by the act of the Christ who continues to lead us now. We were — and we slip back into our former condition so easily — in slavery to the kind of individual and group self-centeredness that cannot face the problems of death and guilt because it always wants life on its own terms. When the phrase "Lamb of God" is used in connection with Jesus, therefore, it refers specifically to this Passover association. We are rescued by his act. He is the Paschal Lamb whose death has saved those who are enabled to identify their needs with him, and the living Lord of those who follow him through death to life.

This kind of Passover-Easter experience is not limited to a particular season associated with the first full moon after the vernal equinox — the traditional way of determining the dates for both festivals. It is continual here and now. As the cross becomes the decisive factor of our meeting any concrete problem — a difficult decision in business life, where we face the problem of our own egotism and the resultant inability to deal with the facts of death and guilt in the problem — we share in new life in Christ. This may not mean success on the world's terms — rather the contrary; but it does mean victorious living in which we are able to trust God's love and face reality for what it is. The resurrection is the only answer for men who are torn by the kind of competition for advancement in industry that leads to ulcers and hypertension for the competers along with "knives in the back" for their opponents; however, it does not guarantee that one will marry the boss's daughter, but rather that he will be able to live in love with himself and his fellow men.

On the night before his arrest, when everybody could see its high probability, if not certainty, Jesus and his disciples met for a "kiddush" meal, in which they broke a piece of bread and shared a cup of wine — something they may have done a good many times before. But this time it had special significance. The kiddush was a common rabbinic custom, in which the rabbi would first bless the bread and the cup before sharing them, thanking God for the kind of fellowship he had with his closest disciples, and suggesting that this association was as important as food and drink — the necessities of life. On this last kiddush, Jesus said, " Do this in remembrance of me."

After he had been arrested, tried, and crucified, the discouraged, disillusioned, frightened group met in loyal allegiance to their dead leader before scattering to their homes to resume if possible their former ways of life. It would have been wonderful if what this leader had stood for could have become the way of the world but such was not to be so. But they held a memorial kiddush, and in this setting the resurrection faith was born. This memorial kiddush became then the first Holy Communion, and the Holy Communion is the distinctive rite of the resurrection fellowship.

The most striking note of the resurrection experience was the enthusiasm and sense of corporateness it generated in the group soon to become apostles. The details of their discovery of the power of the living Christ are hard to recapture, but the evidence suggests that their conviction had a Eucharistic focus from the beginning — not that his had been invariable, but that it had been normal. As Cleopas reported to the disciples in Jerusalem, " He was known to us in the breaking of bread."

The resurrection discovery meant to the original group that the destiny of Israel had been fulfilled — that the objective toward which the Jewish tradition of the Law and the Prophets had been aiming for centuries had now been obtained. In other words, according to the imagery they themselves used, it meant that the Lord's Messiah had actually come and in a guise no one expected — not a second David, nor a second Moses, but as the crucified Son of Man, whose living power in the fellowship life of his adherents opened their eyes to see meanings in their tradition which now made sense to them. Thus they took passages such as those referring to the Suffering Servant of Isaiah, ch. 53, probably written about the faithful remnant of Israel centuries earlier, and made them apply to an even more significant faithful remnant of just one person, who fulfilled the law with absolute loyalty by dying on a cross. And this application made sense, not because it was what the original writer in the Old Testament had meant, but rather because it underlined what the first century readers had discovered in their own experience.

The resurrection discovery was that of a new life, shared in immediacy by those who accepted Christ as Lord. It was not only his new life, something beyond description, but theirs in him and his in theirs. No doubt varying opinions about the immediate Second Coming colored the application of this resurrection in the first generation. Its full implications would have to be worked out as the new fellowship encountered unanticipated problems in the course of the next few centuries. But the central reality remained constant and still does. Likewise, the original Eucharistic focus remains vital. Every service of the Holy Communion is as much a resurrection meal as that of the disciples on the Emmaus road.

The new fellowship of those in whose corporate life the presence of the risen Christ was the most sure of sure realities would face many difficulties, in the course of which new aspects to their discovery would become clear. The resurrection faith was discovered within a generation or so to obliterate the distinction between Jew and Gentile on the part of those within the Church, but by so doing it would draw a new and sharp line between the new Israel and the old. Those who would have tolerated a minor Jewish sect with special tenets were not prepared to see the traditions of Judaism's unique role in history set aside. The resurrection faith would raise serious problems about the kind of claim an omnicompetent society might make upon its members, and the resulting conflict involving persecution and testing would eventually infiltrate the Empire itself. The resurrection faith would encounter all kinds of people who would seek to borrow it to justify one way or another of solving problems through evasion — first century Gnosticism, twentieth century Christian Science — and would have come to a clear understanding of Christian responsibility in the world of history. Eventually becoming the dominant religion of Europe, the faith would be tested by attempts to exploit it in the service of political goals and social solidarity. It would face internal struggles, misunderstandings, and bitterness. But one thing would remain constant — to the extent that men and women knew the resurrection faith itself with any reality, they would themselves be changed persons with a new and fresh appreciation of their relationship to the Lord God of the universe through Christ Jesus his Son, and a sense of brotherhood with the family of the children of God.

The heart of the Christian proclamation of the resurrection is Paul's statement to the Colossians: "If ye then be risen with Christ, seek those things which are above, where Christ sitteth on the right hand of God." The man who uses death as the gateway to life, and who denies his own self-righteousness in his effort to do the best he can where he is, finds himself reborn as adequate to meet the new demands of a changing world. Dealing with man's understanding of the meaning of his whole life, the Christian affirmation is that those who have accepted without evasion their own problems of guilt and death, and who have interpreted these problems in the light of the cross, are enabled to live creatively here and now.

The meaning of the resurrection for men and women who are trying to make sense out of their own lives, and interpret their needs for security, status, and achievement in an honest, realistic way, is that when they meet decisions — practical decisions — in the spirit of the cross, they themselves are reborn. It is this kind of appreciation of a new relationship to life's problems that makes men like Paul cry out, "Not I live, but Christ Jesus, he liveth in me." This is not a poetic flight of fancy, but an interpretation of life's meaning, which, if it has any relevance at all, describes a man discussing family finances with his wife across the breakfast table, or parents working out with their adolescent children a practical policy as to the use of the family car.

What happened to Jesus is not as important as what happens to those who take the cross into their own hearts. If they have not understood life's meaning on the basis of Jesus' dramatic encounter with guilt and death, their concern with what happened to Jesus is merely speculation. If they have been led to understand their own struggles to make life meaningful, however, in terms of the cross, then they already know all that they care about knowing — that they are risen with Christ, and that they can approach their practical decisions by the way of the cross.

To know the resurrection this way means, for example, that a bereaved person is able to handle his natural feelings of personal guilt and his natural sense of personal loss with serenity and confidence, because his primary awareness is that he can go ahead and make his readjustments trusting God, provided only that he is honest with himself. To know the resurrection this way means that a young couple, recently married, are able to deal gladly and creatively with the fact that each of them is still the same person he was before he was married, with all the same fears and hopes, good habits and bad habits, none of which has been magically changed, but that the venture of faith upon which the two have entered is a really new life before God.

That Jesus foresaw the resurrection in anything like the way the Christian Church understands it is to be doubted, because such a prior understanding would have weakened the meaning of his encounter with guilt and death through the actual crucifixion. That he understood, perhaps gradually, yet with more and more direct sureness, the key to life's meaning is to be presumed. And that key was: Face facts, go ahead, trust God to overrule the result, not according to what we think it ought to be, but according to reality. The cross was the ultimate application of that key in Jesus' own life, and symbolically for ours. The resurrection was its triumphant affirmation in the faith of those who found it available for themselves.

The discovery of the resurrection faith was doubtless the appreciation at first of a few people that they had found the answer, for which all men were looking, in a form that nobody would have guessed. Possibly Peter focused this original insight for his companions. We do not know, and it really makes no difference. Peter, at any rate, became an early interpreter of its meaning. What is important, and what is clear, is that the group of disciples, meeting possibly after the crucifixion to hold a memorial kiddush meal in literal obedience to the command they had heard at the Last Supper — "Do this in remembrance of me" — found a new and unexpected faith.

As they recalled the events, the Passover symbolism was associated with the time of year when the events occurred, and as they recalled Jesus' own living faith, they discovered that they could make his way of facing life their way. This discovery was not simply the acceptance of a new and more profound moral obligation. It was primarily their feeling that when they thought of Jesus as their Christ, they were really facing up to the practical meanings of death and guilt in their own lives. The resurrection is, therefore, first of all the rebirth of living men and women who acquire a new relationship to their problems by making their own, through faith, the spirit of Jesus on the cross. And the witness of those who have done so throughout the ages is the confident assurance that Jesus as the Christ is the strongest living force in the world — not in theory but in practical living. This is realized by people who are empowered to meet more humbly and more creatively their own problems of home, business, and community.

The tendency of the world is to be polytheistic — that is, to see no solution to the confusing, competing, complicated demands of real decisions, involving the problems of guilt and death and threatening security, status, and achievement for all concerned. More thoughtful people find themselves alternating between a Sadducee relationship to these demands, which tries to solve them by individual and group adjustment, and a Pharisee response, which tries to handle them by a formula to which all men can be loyal. The genius of the Christian understanding of life is its recognition of the need for both adjustment and universal loyalty, but going beyond these to the heart of the problem of meaningful living: man's refusal to face fully the causes of his confusion and despair. The cross and resurrection are the practical and vital symbols for the kind of response to life that indicates an adequate religion.

A notice from his draft board, for example, may easily shake a man's understanding of life's meaning because it compels him, whether or not he is willing, to alter his plans and to submit his person to an external regimen. Except for those few who are prepared on the grounds of conscience to take some alternative to military service, the draft summons raises a fundamental religious issue. With those who have chosen the role of the C.O., and with those who are prepared to take up the profession of soldier, the issue has already been faced somewhat and a particular decision has been made in advance, so that the response to the draft notice is primarily a test of sincerity. Most people, however, cannot deal with the problem this way, and for many the conscientious objector seems to be a particularly noble form of Pharisee, with the defects of that religious attitude.

To accept one's draft summons on the basis of the cross and resurrection, however, is a profound religious act. It does not mean a simple resignation to the inevitable, nor does it mean a simple acceptance of war as a desirable instrument of national policy. But it does mean that the changes in a man's way of living are, first of all, not understood egotistically. The forced deferral of education, business career, and possibly marriage do not embitter him. He can be himself in the new situation, accepting it for what it is.

He can, in the second place, see his role in a large perspective, recognizing himself to be a part of the human race, whose fears and suspicions and egotism cause wars. It does not destroy a man's loyalty or interfere with his duty as a soldier for him to understand penitently what he is doing.

In the third place, he can see his relationships to his fellow soldiers and the officers over him with a healthy realism which saves him from wanting to curry favor and also from shirking responsibility, yet allows for an interest in personalities as personalities where circumstances permit.

But, above all, he may live in the faith that he belongs to a brotherhood which is bigger and more important than the divisions between men, and stronger than the conflicts which array men against each other. While he cannot ignore the fact that he is a soldier, and as such is a participant on a particular side, he sees the war, nevertheless, without discounting its reality, horror, and bitterness in the least, against the background of the victorious peace of God in his own heart, in the hearts of other men, and ultimately overruling history itself.

To read one's draft summons in the light of the cross and resurrection, or to accept any other forced decision, is not an easy thing. There is no promise that even with such a reading of the meaning the circumstances will ever be easy or other people in any way responsive. But there is a point of view here that gives the man who has it a purpose greater than circumstances and enables him to live with unsolved difficulties.

CHAPTER VIII

Love — the Impossible Imperative

" YE HAVE not chosen me, but I have chosen you, and ordained you, that ye should go and bring forth fruit, and that your fruit should remain; that whatsoever ye shall ask of the Father in my name, he may give it you. These things I command you, that ye love one another."

These words are a description of the reaction of men and women to contact with Jesus as their Christ. John's Gospel is summing up the faith of the Early Church as to what made life meaningful, glorious, and strong. With more than half a century intervening between the writing of these words and the historical event lying back of the cross and resurrection, the members of that early Christian fellowship could interpret their relationship to Jesus in no other way than that contact with reality which made sense out of life.

The words from John's Gospel give an understanding of life's meaning, the acknowledgment of a demand, and the response of faith. They are not a statement of a theory, however, but the affirmation of living people who had discovered in their own lives the meaning of transforming identification with Jesus as their Lord. In a new and more vital way than they had ever imagined could be possible, these early Christians were convinced that they were really in tune with reality. They could appreciate the fundamental clarity of life's demand upon them, and they knew that this was the way life was meant to be.

The response of those who have accepted Jesus Christ as their Lord, through the crucifixion of their own autonomy, has always been to see in their own hearts the searchlight of truth directed upon the darkness of their world. While no one can claim that everyday problems have been eliminated, nevertheless the response of faith has always included a consciousness of daylight victorious over darkness, and of death being conquered by life. While no one can claim that there are no intellectual difficulties to be faced, nevertheless the response has always included a sense of harmony with the purpose and movement of the universe. While no one can deny that every living person necessarily encounters disappointments and frustrations and sadness, nevertheless the response has always included a triumphant joy which transcends all lesser sorrows, without denying what is real, but pointing to a higher reality.

Paul put the same idea in these words: " For God, who commanded the light to shine out of darkness, hath shined in our hearts, to give the light of the knowledge of the glory of God in the face of Jesus Christ."

A man does not choose to be born. He is born. He becomes aware of his own existence after the fact of birth. His own life is prior to his questions about its meaning. Whatever else may confuse and perplex him, he does not seriously doubt his own existence. Even if he goes through the motions of doing so speculatively, those motions have no real meaning. Man discovers himself called into life. He cannot deny the fact. All he can do is to live and try to interpret what his living means so that he can make sense out of his experience. The demand of life is laid on him before he does anything about it. Man's religious questions are a response to a demand, not the creation of the demand. Reality makes sense in no other way.

The Christian's response to life, once he has accepted Jesus as his Christ, is parallel to the response of natural man to the mere fact of being alive. And he interprets his experience that way. Although man must accept Jesus as his Christ by faith, through identification of his own life with the cross and resurrection, he does not regard that acceptance and identification as manufacturing his own Christ. He regards it as acknowledging the facts of life — as reality itself — and his response will make sense in no other way.

To accept Jesus as one's Christ — that is, to associate one's own struggle with the problems of death and guilt in life's natural transitions and decisions with the cross and resurrection — is to acquire an entirely new relationship to the underlying religious question. The demand of life has been translated into another idiom, which is now understood to be a more profound statement of the requirement of meaningfulness. Whereas all men respond to the demand to make sense out of experience or live in an intolerable situation, without security, status, and achievement, the response of faith to Jesus as the Christ puts the demand in another form. John's Gospel uses these words: " These things I command you, that ye love one another."

As we have seen right along, life's demand is always dynamic and requires a response in the context of practical situations. For men and women who understand life polytheistically, the only conceivable response is a man-centered one, primarily an egocentric one, which by extension may be thought of in terms of the group or class or nation, or even the Church with which the responder is identified. In the last analysis, polytheistic man is engaged in conversation with himself. He is engaged in answering his own questions, with no possibility of any other kind of discourse. He can only arbitrate between conflicting issues in terms of his own interest or advantage or convenience. There is no other possibility.

Men and women who respond to life's demand on the basis of

monotheism do not live by any simple man-centered view of reality. While the transcendent loyalty turns out to be partly a creation of man's own idea of a perfect world, which monotheists believe to be attainable — within the eventual grasp of man — nevertheless this loyalty is also partly a recognition of the Creator God standing over against his creation. Although it is within man's power, someday if not now, to develop an order in which tension and confusion are eliminated, that order is thought of (whether in Marxist or Old Testament sense) as conforming to reality rather than creating reality. Consequently, monotheistic man is not talking to himself. He is talking to an Other. But he is doing all the talking. He is not really listening. It is not a simple monologue, as in the case of polytheistic man, nor is it a true dialogue. It is one-way speech in the presence of a listener.

The result of the Christian encounter, however, is to translate the process of religious question from that of monologue or speech-in-the-presence-of-a-listener to a true dialogue. Man listens and then responds. The prophet Isaiah anticipated this reality, although not quite in the form of a dialogue, in the vision encountered in Isa., ch. 6: " Also I heard the voice of the Lord, saying, Whom shall I send, and who will go for us? Then said I, Here am I; send me." Where the encounter fails to be a true dialogue is in the general, impersonal character of the question the prophet hears. There is no religious ambiguity in the statement the Christian hears addressed to him personally, although it is also addressed to others: " These things I command you, that ye love one another." He responds to the direct demand of life upon him, by saying, " Yes."

The Christian encounter is that of man who realizes that he is a " thou " responding personally to another " I." He is not just a person who figures out that this would, indeed, be a better world if all men did love one another, and, therefore, resolves to try to see what he can do about it. Rather he is a person who feels himself introduced to the inner nature of reality, whereby he is given life's demand in the only possible form that makes sense on the level of history where he lives. He did not create the demand. He knows that it is the demand of truth itself. He does not deceive himself that either he or society, today or sometime in the future, will make the fulfillment of the demand the order of the world. He responds by saying " I " in response to the antecedent " I " of God, because on no other basis can life mean anything.

Love is the impossible imperative. Obviously some actions and some relationships between men are preferable to others, and some seem to reflect the divine imperative more truly than others, but there is a great gulf fixed between man's accomplishments and the divine demand. The Christian is not a person who has in his possession the answers to all questions. He is just a person who has learned through faith the kind of answers he must make to God's question, and hence the direction in which he must search for practical answers. He knows what kind of questions to ask himself, and for him that is enough.

The Christian encounter, like all other religious formulations, has to be carried into the world of everyday affairs and make sense there in the course of the transitions which every man has to make, and the decisions which are forced upon every man for choice. In one sense, the difference might be put this way — whereas ordinary man views every problem of decision and transition as the threat of death and guilt, or both, to his own security, status, and achievement, the man who has accepted Jesus as his Christ sees the same issues as occasions where the demand of God — " love one another " — is the more accurate description of the problem.

It is not that anyone who understands the connection of his own life with the cross and resurrection believes that he is going to fulfill the impossible imperative completely now or ever;

or that he believes that any group, Church, or society will re-capitulate the fulfillment as a historical achievement. It is simply that this is what makes sense, and this is what he wants to do. He understands the reality of death and guilt in the light of the cross and resurrection, and, therefore, knows that his own successes and failures are not the most important issue. It is enough to go ahead in faith, doing the best he can with what he has where he is. The dialogue " I-thou " is only relevant " here and now," because that is where we live.

When men and women confront their own lives with the cross and resurrection, they can make the identification only by faith. On any other terms, their own lives are the antithesis, not the parallel or the equivalent. We are the crucifiers. When anything resembling crucifixion comes our way, we resent it as unmerited and unfair. One cannot appreciate the meaning of the cross and resurrection for himself unless he also appreciates that his own denial of guilt and evasion of death is specifically condemned. He cannot make the identification a matter of personal or group accomplishment. He cannot make it a matter of ritual or form or ethical standard. He can only make it when by faith he uses it as the pattern for his own practical decisions.

Just as it is inconceivable that any individual or group can ever simply re-enact the cross and resurrection as historical events, so also is the case regarding the commandment to love. But the issue is not whether individuals or groups fulfill this commandment in history. It is, rather, whether they understand the meaning of their own individual and group lives in its terms, and so really overcome the threats of death and guilt in practical situations.

The symbols of the cross and resurrection become the means by which the man who has accepted Jesus as his Lord appreciates the meaning of forgiveness as applied to himself. The very contradiction between the cross and resurrection as used by

Jesus, and his own historical and intellectual situation as he approached them, prevents any possibility of literal appropriation. The very idea is preposterous that any individual or any group could seriously conceive of itself as re-enacting the cross and resurrection in real historical situations. The only thing men can do is to identify themselves by faith, and by so doing permit their own autonomy to be crucified that they may be reborn as conscious children of God. This means the acceptance of forgiveness, or else there would be a gulf between man's awareness of his own situation and what the cross and resurrection demonstrate. The denial of self-righteousness by Jesus on the cross and his refusal to demand personal vindication made possible the forgiving contact. Forgiveness involves identification on the basis of mutual recognition of the facts between the forgiver and the forgiven. For the man and woman who have identified themselves by faith with the cross and resurrection of Jesus Christ the awareness of being forgiven is the most real of awarenesses. And the forgiveness is not separated from, but part of, the unconditioned "I-thou" demand, experienced in personal dialogue.

The impossible imperative — the love commandment — is that direction of living by which men and women live as forgiven persons, applying what they take to be life's meaning in practical situations. The issue of their own perfection is not important. The only issue is to live as a forgiven person, reflecting the forgiving love. The love commandment is the fundamental description of how we reflect the "I-thou" dialogue with God by appreciating the reality and significance of "I-thou" relationships with other people here and now. But this is only possible for those who feel a personal share in the cross and resurrection and hence know themselves to be forgiven people. In other words, the commandment to "love one another" is for Christians the description of the meaning of individual and group life as it is encountered in the course of life's natural transitions, and the decisions we are forced to make. Paul describes it as " I live; yet not I, but Christ liveth in me."

Every person who takes his relationships with others seriously knows the problem for which the impossible imperative is the answer. Every parent concerned about his children, every husband and wife concerned about each other, every citizen concerned about his responsibility, every employer concerned about those who work for him — all these know the way practical issues contradict their ethical ideals. People who take life's demands seriously are forced into the position of either deceiving themselves that they are already meeting their concerns adequately, or of despairing of being able to respond at all. Every conscientious parent certainly knows the temptation to meet his children's needs by some type of formula, and also the moods which come so often when he wonders whether he can ever be adequate at all. To those who understand what Paul meant when he wrote: " For the good that I would, I do not; but the evil which I would not, that I do. . . . O wretched man that I am! who shall deliver me from the body of this death?," the Christian faith gives the same answer today that it gave to him, " Thanks be to God, which giveth us the victory through our Lord Jesus Christ."

There has been a growing awareness of the responsibility of the Church and the school to train young people for marriage. Ministers and teachers have taught the economics of marriage, the sociology of marriage, and the biology of marriage; but not too much has been done with the theology of marriage. Yet what young couples need in working through their adjustments is something more than factual data and techniques, important as they are. What they need to know is that life's meaning, in marriage, does not depend merely upon their own good intentions, which turn out to be frail reeds upon which to lean.

Rather, the fulfillment of marriage is in forgiveness, as they understand themselves and each other to be mere human beings with all the frailty of men, and, on the other hand, those who have been joined together by a common faith, in which they are able to trust God to complete their incompleteness.

Forgiveness, therefore, refers to the practical relationships of living people, whose decisions involve their homes, businesses, neighborhoods, communities, and nation. Where the Sadducee attitude is often a counsel of despair, and the Pharisee attitude forces one to deceive himself in order to keep going in a world where one's ideals are being continually denied by one's own actions, the Christian attitude makes possible both realistic and victorious living. For a man to regard himself as forgiven, through the cross of Christ, does not mean to regard himself as perfect. It does not mean that the moral battle is over, now or ever. It does mean that he can keep on going, provided he is honest with himself, recognizing his own inadequacy and self-blinded vision. As he does the best he can, with what he has, where he is, he trusts God to complete his incompleteness, not because of his righteousness or wisdom, but because life makes sense that way. This is the attitude of acceptance of the impossible imperative which makes it possible to meet the problems of death and guilt.

There is all the difference in the world between the love commandment and a systematic ethic. Attempts to make it the root principle of moral law end by turning Christianity back into Pharisaism and depriving the cross and resurrection of religious meaning. The ethical requirements of life remain what the world in its evolution has discovered them to be — particularly as illuminated by the Old Testament, and as sharpened by contemporary social issues. Jesus said: "Think not that I am come to destroy the law, or the prophets: I am come not to destroy, but to fulfil." One does not need a Christian faith to amplify the ethic.

The ethic has already been stated in such noble terms that if men were other than they are and history other than it is, we should have all the moral guidance necessary for a very adequate life. Merely adding to the ethical requirements serves no real purpose, even though most people need to have their moral horizons widened. What the love commandment does is to state the foundations of life for those who are "risen with Christ," the premises upon which they live, the directions which they assume. The connection with the ethic is primarily through the elimination of tension between men and the ethical demands they know they ought to accept. But death and guilt are really overcome through faith and forgiveness, not through the elimination of moral problems.

When men and women accept the cross and resurrection as the description of life's meaning, they are then freed to deal with life's problem with relative objectivity. Freedom from slavery to death and guilt is possible only through faith and forgiveness. The love commandment is the description of freedom. He who is the prisoner of Christ, through the crucifixion of his own autonomy, is no longer on the defensive against other people and no longer fears life's transitions, nor feels impelled to run away from decisions. This is what it means to be "the prisoner of the Lord."

The love commandment is the description of that understanding of one's own religious needs which enables a man to go ahead in faith. This is the basis upon which he can make sense of experience. This is, therefore, the description of reality from the religious point of view.

The distinctive description of the Early Christian Church, as given in the book of The Acts, is that "they [the new converts] continued steadfastly in the apostles' doctrine and fellowship, and in breaking of bread, and in prayers." In everyday life, the breaking of bread is the mark of the family dinner table, and where do people normally find both acceptance and forgiveness more naturally, as part of the way life goes on, than in their families? In other words, the love commandment suggests that the Christian faith is to be found in the family life of the people of God. And the family meal, which we now know as the Holy Communion, is the sacramental side of the same thing — we become a family through contact with our Lord at his table, so that we may go back into the world to live as the sons of God and as brothers of one another. Of course, we do not do this fully or consistently, yet we see the need and we also know the power of God to use even our feeble efforts. So we return again and again to the Holy Table to the "breaking of bread" so that the love commandment may again speak with power to our hearts.

As given in the Gospels of Matthew, Mark, and Luke, and used traditionally in the teaching of the Christian Church, the love commandment is always stated in the double form — "Thou shalt love the Lord thy God with all thy heart, and with all thy soul, and with all thy mind," and "Thou shalt love thy neighbor as thyself." These are not two commandments, and there is certainly no tension between the two expressions. In the double form, they are obverse and reverse of each other like the two sides of a coin. The result of accepting Jesus as Christ is not assuming two new obligations, but accepting a relationship to reality in its totality — both its ultimate and its immediate demands — which may be characterized by love. The relationship of the Christian toward God is in terms of a dialogue involving the whole of life's meaning, where the description "I-thou" means personal encounter, with man the willing listener. The relationship of the Christian with his neighbor is in terms of a dialogue also — but this time dealing only with certain details, yet these details epitomize life's meaning. In both cases — the encounter with the ultimate demand and the encounter with the immediate situation — faith and forgiveness have established a new relationship, and death and guilt are overcome.

For Christians, the love commandment in both its single and double form is the description of man's acceptance of life's demand, as he understands that demand in the light of the cross and resurrection. Without the prior event of the cross, the love commandment is just an idealization of ethical obligation. When it is accepted as the description of life's meaning, however, because Jesus is the Christ, men can say with John, "We love him, because he first loved us."

When the demand of the impossible imperative is taken seriously, and the cross and resurrection are seen as the only means for fulfilling it, then we discover that life's relationships may be put in the form of a triangle. At the one corner is God, at another our brother, and at the third the self of each individual or the collective self with which he may be identified at the moment. It does not make any difference where one enters the triangle, nor in which direction one goes around it. It means the same thing — from God through my brother to me, from God through me to my brother; from my brother through God to me, from my brother through me to God; from me through God to my brother, from me through my brother to God.

CHAPTER IX

The Relevant Description of Life

THE Christian faith has to stand the tests of life in exactly the same manner in which any other religion, formal or informal, explicit or implicit, has to meet them. The Christian religion exists as a force in the world because some men and women have been convinced that identification of themselves with Jesus on the cross has made it possible for them to deal adequately with death and guilt. The Christian religion derives its relevance from the conviction of some men and women that, since they are themselves forgiven sinners, they have a new relationship to practical affairs.

The test of any religious statement is whether it actually makes it possible for men and women to interpret life's meaning honestly and realistically under strains of varying intensity. Its theoretical consistency and logical argument are of little value if people are not able to use it to make life meaningful when they are under pressure. The Christian faith, which claims to go to the heart of life's problems instead of being cut short like the halfway solutions of the Pharisees and the Sadducees, has to prove its claims in real circumstances if they are to be more than words.

While a particular interpretation of living may appear to be relatively adequate to those who have been directly subjected to some tremendously illuminating experience, no religious statement can serve the function of religion very long unless it is capable of being transmitted by the original group to other people. The real test comes when later generations, who have undergone cultural changes and as a result speak a somewhat different language, try to use it. If a religious statement is to be useful over long periods of history, it must demonstrate practical relevance to the perennial problems of human nature — to those issues which continue in individual and group experience despite the rise and fall of civilization. Christianity cannot avoid this test either. Their contact with the cross may have been the supremely vital religious insight for Peter and the other disciples, and for men of unusual imagination who lived in the same culture, such as Paul, but that does not prove that the cross would serve the same purpose for other men of other cultures of later times.

No expression of religion can meet the tests of life very long if it is primarily dependent on verbal statements. Words tend to be time-conditioned as to meaning. Figures of speech grow out of the cultural situations in which people live. The slang of a half century ago is almost meaningless today to people who read it in old books. The more serious descriptions of human experience may have a much longer life because that to which they refer changes in significance more slowly, but all verbal descriptions have to meet the test of obsolescence. One of the great difficulties, for instance, in much modern economic thought has been the tradition of trying to use the understanding of Adam Smith, which was very apt for the age in which he wrote, in order to interpret very different conditions. A religion that is dependent on words alone is continually under the threat of becoming obsolete through irrelevance — if its statements are too concrete, that which they describe may disappear; and if they are too general or abstract, they will lose vitality as time puts distance between the statements and the experiences that gave rise to them.

In other words, if a religion is to remain vital and to serve as the basis by which men reach satisfying understandings about security, status, and achievement, it must express itself through symbols, concrete enough to be directly personal and universal enough to continue meaningful as long as human nature remains as it is. The cross is such a symbol. One might put its message into words — either into a narrative telling how people use its approach to life in the practical situations of home and community or into a philosophical discourse on its meaning — but if its religious value depends on words alone, it cannot continue to meet the functional tests. While the symbol cannot serve any purpose unless it is continually stated in words by each generation, as each wrestles with the problem of religion in the particular circumstances of its age, the symbol cannot depend on any one statement.

The cross and resurrection are living realities which each age must interpret for itself as men and women wrestle with the problems of guilt and death. To the extent to which they are led to ask the most significant and penetrating questions of life's meaning — significant and penetrating not in an involved philosophical sense, but in a practical sense — they will find the cross and resurrection to be adequate symbols. The purpose of a religious symbol is to enable men and women to interpret their own situations with realism and with creative purpose, helping them to sense realities that otherwise elude their grasp, and to go in directions that otherwise cannot be defined. The symbols that do this have vitality, and qualify functionally as the bearers of a religious insight that can stand the tests of death and guilt without self-deception, illusion, or evasion. The symbols of a vital religion, therefore, as has been said before, speak a language of the heart at the same time that they are expressed in intellectual forms, and this language of the heart is the significant thing. It is the claim of Christian faith that the cross and resurrection belong to this language of the heart, which remains relevant age after age although customs change.

The Christian faith claims to stand the tests of life and to be just as relevant in the twentieth century as it was in the first. It is obvious, however, to any realistic observer that a great deal of what passes for Christianity has become primarily the retention of time-honored traditional religious acts and customs, which have little if any relevance to the way men understand their own problems and the problems of their world. It is doubtful whether many serious thinkers — as against those who tend to use naïve oversimplifications in their reaction to pressure — really use Christian symbols, as such, as the means by which they interpret for themselves the struggles they are actually facing in their private, personal lives, and in their world. Very few psychiatrists have discovered that the cross and resurrection are the most profound symbols that patients can be guided to use as the means of understanding their problems and asking realistic, functional questions about life. While Christianity may claim to meet the tests, it is often used in the same manner that an antique chair is preserved in a museum. Although it may be beautiful to look at and rich in historical associations, it is not serving the purpose of a chair because it has a cord stretched across the front to prevent anyone from sitting in it.

It is to be expected that particular expressions of the basic Christian symbols will be gradually discarded, while new ones are developed. The danger is that the underlying symbol may likewise come to be regarded as irrelevant. In the early days of the Christian movement, there was a widely followed custom of centering fellowship life in a community supper called the agape, or love feast. In the days of persecution, when a large percentage of the adherents of the new faith were underprivileged people, this custom functionally dramatized what they meant by the spirit of brotherhood in Christ. It was more than a means of giving people something to eat. But with the recognition of Christianity as legal and with its acceptance as the official religion of the culture, the agape lost its significance because it was not needed in the same way. Yet it has been difficult for the average Christian ever since to feel as fresh and vital a participation in a brotherhood "where there is neither Greek nor Jew, . . . Barbarian, Scythian, bond nor free" as apparently men felt when the agape was developed. The same kind of claim has been made, and made much more fully and dramatically, for the Eucharist or Holy Communion, but it is doubtful whether the practical application of the resurrection to life has ever been so clear.

The Christian fellowship has always been more or less aware of the problem of obsolescence, just as it has always been aware, at least unconsciously, that the cross and resurrection are significant primarily in a functional sense. In the very earliest days of experimental use of these symbols as means of dealing with the problems of guilt and death, and of asking the most penetrating questions about life's meaning, the possibility was naturally raised that perhaps this new understanding of life's direction had only limited use. There were those who tried to restrict it to the Jewish community as such, regarding it primarily as a refinement, an improvement, on Pharisee religion. There were those who, in a lower-class Sadducee way, tried to use it to get rid of their own inhibitions without thinking any further about its significance. There were those who appreciated somewhat its value in dealing with both guilt and death simultaneously without ignoring one or the other, but who wondered whether it could possibly do this for people who had not been associated personally with Jesus, or whether it would have any meaning away from the historical setting of the original experiences in Palestine.

As an answer to these natural questions, which would, however, water down the meaning of the cross and resurrection and weaken, if not entirely destroy, the functional value of these symbols for dealing with death and guilt, the early Christian fellowship developed two companion symbols, of lesser importance certainly but of great usefulness. While we have inherited these symbols as if they were appreciated completely at the beginning of the life of the Christian fellowship, they must have been developed experimentally, even though the original statement of each was necessarily a flash of insight. As we know them today, however, these companion symbols have become for many people so institutionalized as to confuse their meaning.

The companion symbols, designed to answer the problem of obsolescence and to demonstrate the universal relevance of the Christian faith, were those of the Ascension and Pentecost. Together they state that Christianity, used as a religion, enables men and women to ask accurate questions of life, and hence to go forward with a sense of purpose. These two symbols are dramatic ways of demonstrating that the way that death and guilt are dealt with by the cross and resurrection of Jesus Christ is what the whole race of man is looking for. They emphasize the universal relevance of the Christian faith as the basis for a realistic appreciation of security, status, and achievement. They assert that the Christian understanding of life's meaning will continue to be adequate, when used functionally, regardless of the intellectual difficulties men have to face or the historical problems in which they become involved. In other words, these two symbols demonstrate the continuing relevance of the Christian faith.

Historically, the Ascension and Pentecost were understandings which originated in the same general reaction of Jesus' most intimate associates to his execution, and which led these men to discover the meaning of the cross and resurrection for their own lives. New Testament scholars generally believe that Easter,

Ascension, and Pentecost are variations on the same theme. Be that as it may, both subsidiary symbols refer to the total Christian encounter with death and guilt. While both are rooted in the experience of Jesus on the cross and the appreciation of that event by those who are identified with him in the resurrection, each has its own distinctive emphasis, and each answers specific questions which may be raised about the functional adequacy of the Christian faith as the religion by which men may truly live.

Both the Ascension and Pentecost are rooted in the dynamic transition experiences which saw the little group of discouraged disciples, who had been confused about the meaning of Jesus' mission, become the apostles. Both point to two sides of what it means to become a Christian and to be a Christian. Both refer to the revolution in human personality which takes place when the power of God overcomes the egotism of man. Both refer to the kind of relationship to God and to one's brothers in which this revolution can take place and in which its results can be maintained. In other words, both eventually refer to the life in love, in which men can accept each other because they are confident that God in Christ has accepted them despite their failings, and in which men dare to forgive each other because they dare to ask forgiveness in the faith that God in Christ forgives the sinners who turn to him. Above all, both refer to that relationship in which the unlovely become lovable because they find it possible to become loving, since they know themselves to be supported by the love of God in the fellowship of those who share the same essential experience and discover the same fundamental relationship to be the key to the new life.

Both the Ascension and Pentecost refer to a relationship which may perhaps be best illustrated by a wheel. The spokes draw nearer to each other as they draw nearer to the hub. In Christ, we find ourselves to be spokes, not separate sticks. At one end we have our several responsibilities in the world, with the unique equipment with which each of us is endowed to handle them. At the other end we are part of a unifying process which relates us purposefully to the common center, from which comes the moving power — transmitted from God through Christ to us. In this sense, if it does not stretch the illustration too much, the rim becomes the Church, which ties together the purpose of the hub and the functions of the spokes in the processes of ongoing life.

The Ascension is the symbol that relates the Christian affirmation of life's meaningfulness to the whole world of human thought. It is a pictorial way of stating, first, that reality stands in judgment on whatever men may think, whether or not they can fit everything together in a logical system. For instance, whatever we may think of child psychology, our theories and our grasp of other people's theories are under the judgment of living situations when our children are concerned, where the point is not to prove or disprove a theory but to deal adequately with the needs of a child. The ascension rests upon the premise that reality takes primacy over thinking whenever the two are in apparent conflict — not that thinking is unimportant, but that its capacity is relative.

The Ascension is the dramatic way in which the Christian faith affirms that the cross and resurrection are expressions of reality itself. Hence they are in judgment upon whatever men may think about them. The important consideration is whether living people are actually able to make sense out of their lives by means of these central symbols so that they are able to handle the problems of security, status, and achievement realistically whatever may happen to them. If they know this to be their own basis for living, that fact takes primacy over all speculation. If they do not know this to be their basis for living, they will never acquire it through philosophy.

The real issue, once human problems are put in this perspective, is not whether men and women are able to figure out completely the theoretical significance of Jesus for the human race, or whether they agree or disagree with propositions of Christian theology. The real issue is whether they understand the meaning of their own lives in terms of the cross and resurrection, and whether they have really encountered the full significance of the problems of guilt and death in their own practical affairs. The cross and resurrection are just as subject to intellectual examination as any other human experience. But they cannot be proved or disproved by intellectual means. For the spectator, looking in from the outside, a question mark will always remain. For the men and women who have discovered the relevance of the Christian affirmation to their own experience, all thinking is preceded by the assertion, such as the blind man made in John's Gospel, "One thing I know, that, whereas I was blind, now I see."

Since the Christian description of man's perennial religious problem is rooted in the very structure of reality itself — this is the way life works when men are content to be themselves in the world as it happens to be — it is inconceivable that any developments in the world of philosophy should ever make the central Christian awareness untrue. The explanations and applications of the cross and resurrection are indeed subject to the limitations of the human intellect, and as such may easily be rendered obsolete as the frontiers of knowledge are pushed back. But the central reality itself is above such contingency. The wisest philosopher, the most learned scientist, the busiest man of affairs, and the humblest peasant may alike find the cross and resurrection of Jesus Christ a sufficient statement of the way to meaningful living for himself, and as such find it intellectually satisfying.

Pentecost is the symbolic way of asserting that the Christian affirmation will continue to be relevant regardless of what happens on the level of history. The Christian interpretation of life's meaning will be an adequate method of dealing with guilt and death regardless of political and economic systems, and regardless of changes in individual fortune. Those who know at first hand what it is to define the meaning of their own lives, and to ask their questions of the universe by means of the cross and resurrection, know themselves to be at one spiritually with all others who are making the same definition, and this unity of attitude transcends all historical changes and differences between men. It does not mean that men can understand one another easily where practical problems are concerned if they view these problems from opposite ends. Americans and Russians are conditioned by their historical positions in evaluating international relations, and are not to be expected to see things alike. Representatives of management and labor are likewise conditioned when it comes to questions of industrial policy. The Pentecostal symbol states dramatically that the Christian affirmation is relevant to people on both sides of historical problems, no matter how serious those problems may be, and that the proof of relevance is in the spirit of fellowship which transcends their differences and transforms their relationship to their problems.

Since the Christian affirmation is rooted in reality and transcends the time-conditioned effects of local circumstance, there is no human situation to which it is not applicable. The justification of missions is not in theoretical claims about the superiority of Christian theory to other religious theories, but in the practical results of Christian faith, which enables men and women of backgrounds and cultures to make sense out of life for themselves in a way nothing else does. When this is understood, practical distinctions can be drawn between the essential and the unessential elements in the Christian missionary enterprise. Since the real issue is for everyone to make sense out of life, the missionary himself can learn from the simpler responses of those to whom the gospel is brought. Thus Western Protestantism has learned the practical lessons of unity from the more literal and practical faith of its converts in South India — and the lesson is not simply one of institutional administration, but one of meeting the threats of guilt and death in ecclesiastical corporate life.

The cross and resurrection were adequate symbols for meaningful living for the depressed classes of the Roman Empire, but they were not limited in meaningfulness to those cultural conditions. In spite of the problems of forced and halfway conversions in the Germanic succession states to the Roman Empire, the Christian affirmation still enabled men and women living under very different circumstances to ask meaningful questions about their own destinies. In the Middle Ages, the Christian faith was not confined to, although it was expressed in, the theory of the corporate society of feudalism. It was able to be stated with new and practical freshness in the Reformation, when the changing conditions of the world rendered the old social structures useless. It can be stated with just as practical relevance today.

The meaning of Pentecost is that Christian understanding of life's meaning, when understood to be an expression of reality, rather than the institutional life of some time-conditioned application of it, is continually relevant to all men, of all ages, of all times, and that they all may know one common central faith despite differences in detail. The meaning of Pentecost is a continual judgment upon all attempts that men make to confine the Christian tradition to one Church system in particular, either in the belief that here is the only valid expression or in the contrary belief that the Christian statement should be rejected because of the errors of one organization. The meaning of Pentecost is that men and women may find the cross and resurrection to be adequate symbols for stating their own problems, for dealing with the pressures of guilt and death, for handling their needs for security, status, and achievement, regardless of changing circumstances, and the test is one of reality, and the experience is one of a faith not limited, but universal.

Pentecost in practice means that the Christian interpretation of life may be meaningful to any to whom the problems of guilt and death are meaningful — whether adolescents, or young married people, or the heads of families, or older men and women. It means that the same basic interpretation can be used by those upon whom fortune smiles and those beset with economic and social and physiological problems. It means that people with different educational backgrounds and different cultures and different tongues can speak the same spiritual language because they face ultimate reality in the same way — and it means that they may know this spiritual unity to be true.

It is the assertion of the Christian faith that it enables men and women to ask the accurate question about life's meaning and so to head their individual and group lives in the right direction. The associated symbols of the Ascension and Pentecost dramatize the universal relevance of this assertion — for our day as for yesterday, and also for tomorrow. While the interpretation will have to be stated in detail in the thought-forms of a particular age and a particular place, and it will have to be applied through particular methods and particular institutions, it is greater than any interpretation or application, and continues to be relevant for all men, for all time, for all the world.

CHAPTER X

The New Order of the Ages

THE vision of John in the book of The Revelation of the New Jerusalem " coming down from . . . heaven, prepared as a bride adorned for her husband," is a poetic way of stating what all thoughtful and sensitive people have always hoped for. Men have always dreamed and planned and worked for a " new order " in which " there shall be no more death, neither sorrow, nor crying, neither shall there be any more pain: for the former things are passed away."

Every great achievement of the human conscience has been understood to be a reflection of this hope — whether it be religious, political, or economic. The great seal of the United States, printed on all one-dollar bills, carries the Latin inscription *Novus Ordo Seclorum.* The designers of the great seal knew that behind the actual accomplishments and failures of the political and economic life of this country there is a dream. Somehow the basic principles of American democracy are felt to be related to the eternal scheme of things. Implied in the motto " The New Order of the Ages " is the belief that this country in its social life demonstrates a fundamental revision of man's traditional way of conducting his affairs, and this change places him in tune with the universe.

Without commenting on the theological accuracy of the dollar bill, we can recognize in that Latin phrase one more expression of the perennial hope of mankind for that kind of society which will make it possible for all men to attain an adequate security, status, and achievement for themselves, and where they will be freed from external threats to their well-being. Men's hopes are always related to the concrete circumstances of their lives — the political and economic context as they know it, their problems of home management, employment, and community adjustment. But these immediate concrete details, which are the practical framework for human life, only focus men's hopes. They do not tell the whole story.

The expression *"Novus Ordo Seclorum"* is essentially religious. It refers implicitly to a new relationship between men and society, between men and things, and between men and themselves, which will transform life's meaning. The only *Novus Ordo* worth having is one in which the problems of death and guilt are dealt with adequately, since unless they are met no circumstantial solution can be more than tentative, and no attainment of security, status, and achievement can be fully satisfactory.

All men are looking for a relationship to life's basic demands that will be clear and meaningful, and will make it possible for them to know where they are going, at least in terms of direction. Their internal drives and the pressures of external circumstances are continually confusing this relationship, because the demands of life are never clear and objective in themselves, but are always understood in terms of the faith by which they live. This means that the hope of the world for a *Novus Ordo Seclorum* is really the hope for such a clarification of men's relationships to life's fundamental demands as will solve permanently the problem of life's meaning.

The Christian faith claims to introduce just this new order of the ages — but not in a sense that disposes of life's problems once and for all, so that no further thought or effort is required of people. The Christian faith claims to introduce the new order

in the sense that men who share it in their hearts are equipped
to deal with the problems of guilt and death as they arise in the
course of man's psychological life and in the historical situations
in which he finds himself involved. It is the assertion of the
Christian faith that the cross and resurrection can be used as the
essential principles by which everyone can understand his own
life, his own relationships to his world, and the significance of
the decisions he is called upon to make.

The Christian faith goes on to clarify what it means in intro-
ducing the new order of the ages by using the symbol of the
Ascension to demonstrate that this kind of relationship to life will
never be intellectually extraneous, no matter how far back the
frontiers of knowledge are pushed, and no matter what distinctions in intellectual capacity are drawn between people; and
it uses the symbol of Pentecost to demonstrate that no historical
or cultural development will ever be beyond its scope or make
it unnecessary. The new order is universal in its range and application. Since all men fundamentally face the same problems
of meaningfulness, regardless of their knowledge or their social
circumstances, and since all societies, regardless of their differences in technics, are subject to the same laws of evolution, the
new order deals with that which is abiding in human nature,
rather than being tied to that which is transitory. But it deals
with it in a way that is practical and applicable to the real
problems men face in a real world.

The Christian faith claims to introduce the new order. Theo-
logically speaking, the name of this new order is the doctrine of
the Trinity. The Trinity refers to man's understanding of God,
hence, to man's understanding of the demands he feels life laying
upon him. Since he can find an adequate religion only to the
extent to which his relationship to these demands is clarified, the
doctrine of the Trinity turns out to be such a clarification, making
it possible for men and women to make sense out of their ex-

perience. Whereas the Sadducee tried to use compromise and adjustment as the principle of clarification, and ended up making himself God in an existential sense, if not in theory, and whereas the Pharisee tried to use a formula calling for universal loyalty as a clarification, and ended up either in self-deception or frustration without the unified demand being fulfilled, the Christian has a basically different understanding.

Although men are aware of life's demands just because they are alive, these demands will always be contradictory and confusing because of human nature and the way history works. But when a man understands life's meaning through the lens, so to speak, of Jesus Christ, he has a different relationship to life's pressures, both internal and external. The Christian faith does not claim that man lives in a perfect world, nor that he lives in a world where he can know how to solve his problems. It does claim, however, that he lives in a world where life now makes sense, and where, despite the unforeseeable nature of many of the demands he meets, he can relate them all to an abiding sense of purpose for himself and for fellowship with others.

In its understanding of man's religious problem, the Pharisee insight saw the necessity of some supreme loyalty serving as the formula by which the confusion of life could be dispelled and the contradiction reduced to harmony. But the Pharisee necessarily has to think of this loyalty in terms of law, in terms of obligation. It does not fulfill itself. He can see only a very clear alternative — without the supreme loyalty, life is chaos; with it, life can be meaningful, provided one is truly loyal. In other words, Pharisee religion cannot really conceive of a God of love. It can conceive only of a God of law and judgment. Even though the great Pharisee leader Hillel used the concept of love in his teaching, it was love as the supreme law rather than as a transforming reality. Men ought to love. By loving one another they fulfilled the supreme loyalty; by loving God they acknowledged the supreme loyalty. But the underlying problem of Pharisaic religion remained just the same as in our discussion of it.

The Christian faith in no way denies the reality of law, nor eliminates obligation. What it does do is to claim to transform men's relationships to the demands of life, and, supremely, to the unconditioned demand of God, overarching all other demands. It claims to make possible that loyalty in terms of spirit and desire, which otherwise exist only on the level of obligation: "This ye ought to do." Men who know themselves to be forgiven sinners through identification with the cross and resurrection are actually new men.

God is known as creator, as supreme ruler of the universe, as moral overlord of history, without any Christian insight being necessary. We have used the tradition of the Pharisees as the noblest human understanding of this kind of recognition. But God cannot be known as Father, and certainly not as loving, unless man's relationship to the demand is transformed from one of obligation to one of desire. Only forgiven sinners, who do not deceive themselves about their own accomplishments or capacity, can use the term with meaning.

The "divinity of Christ" has been argued backward and forward in terms of abstractions ever since the first century. For genuine Christian faith, which responds to reality, there never has been a problem of fact, even though there have been many problems about the best way of describing the fact. When the symbol of "divinity" is used in a functional sense, it is the reaction of men and women who know in their own experience the truth of John's dictum: "No man hath seen God at any time; the only begotten Son, which is in the bosom of the Father, he hath declared him." The reason that Jesus is called the only-begotten Son, the reason that Jesus is called divine, the reason for the centrality of Jesus in Christian faith, is not a matter of theory. It is because men and women who have found the cross and resurrection to be the basis upon which they themselves could handle their own problems of death and guilt have felt that their relationship to life's central demand was clarified thereby.

Without a Son, there is no Father. The first and second Persons of the Trinity are symbols which require each other in order to make sense at all. The God of monotheism is not a loving Father, but a creator, a judge, a lawgiver. Man obeys or dies, and that is all there is to it. Man conforms or lives in a meaningless world, and that is that. But when men and women come to grips with the religious problem by using the symbols of the cross and resurrection to describe the meaning of their own lives, the whole situation is changed. They are no longer on the defensive against life. They are ready to face up to the problem of their own autonomy drive. They are willing to accept the significance of death and guilt in human decisions. They know, in principle, what it is to say, " I live; yet not I, but Christ liveth in me."

The second Person of the Trinity is in a sense the first, since it is by contact with Jesus as the Christ that men find their relationship to life's demands transformed. But he really dramatized reality and also the way to meet it. The demand exists with or without Jesus. The need for a unified interpretation of experience exists whether or not anything makes it possible. The first Person is first in the sense that we did not make the world — it was given. All we can do is live in it and interpret it and make some contribution to it. But it is through Jesus as the Christ that we come into such a relationship to life's unconditioned demand that all other things are given a place and all lesser demands are seen in proportion.

But the transforming experiences of the cross and the resurrection are never simply once-and-for-all events for living men and women. They are the symbols by which men and women define the meaning of their lives in the actual decisions and transitions they have to make. Death and guilt are never disposed of once and for all. Every decision and every transition raises the question again. As long as real people live in a real world they will have to come to terms with problems they cannot foresee, and they will have to do something about their past mistakes.

While the cross and resurrection, as symbols of functional religion, do not eliminate the problem of later transitions in the course of normal living, and the unforeseeable decisions which everyone is called upon to make, they do create a bond of fellowship between men and women who have understood what it means to accept Jesus as the Christ. Men and women never face decisions as if they themselves were blank pieces of paper to be written on for the first time, and they never interpret the transitions of normal living in a social vacuum. Life's meaning is always partly understood — and a large part at that — in a social way, even though everyone makes his own decisions for himself. The prevailing culture defines the general meaning of normal transitions for its members. When we realize that so many of our decisions are made upon very questionable premises, and that we take these premises for granted because they are generally accepted by the groups in which we move, we realize how important for religious purposes is our understanding of the kind of community of people to which we belong. The Christian faith claims to create a new community for those who accept it, and claims that this new community transcends the divisions of race and class and nation and language and educational background which separate men from one another. It does not ignore these divisions, but it gives men and women the awareness of a new environment in which to make their decisions and to interpret life's transitions, and it gives them the support of a fellowship of people whose lives are built upon the same basically transforming religious experience.

In other words, although it is impossible to put one's Christian faith "on ice," so to speak, so that one no longer has to deal with any problem of death and guilt, there is another side of the picture. While our need for adequate security, status, and achievement is perennial, and our consciousness of it is awakened every time we face an important problem, nevertheless, we do not face these problems cold. The Christian is aware that the cross and resurrection are symbols which must be seen in every significant living situation in which he finds himself, but he makes that recognition in the fellowship of those who share the same understanding of what is involved in meaningful living.

When the Creeds mention the Holy Ghost, and when the concept of the Trinity is used to demonstrate that this third aspect of Deity is just as essential for a complete and adequate faith as the other two, the following is what is meant. The doctrine of the Trinity is the symbolic way of recognizing that men are given a transformed relationship to the unconditioned demand through identifying their religious needs with the cross and resurrection of Jesus Christ. This gives them the assurance that they live in an essentially benign universe, but, at the same time, this faith to be real must be applied daily in life's practical decisions; and it can be so applied with power in the fellowship of those who share the same interpretation of life's meaning. The doctrine of the Holy Spirit is just as significant an aspect of the Christian understanding of adequate religion as are the other elements, since it is in terms of the continued decision and the continuing fellowship that the Christian faith remains relevant for human needs.

The Gospel of John devotes three chapters to discourses in which the Holy Spirit is related to Christian discipleship. Since the first seventeen chapters of this Gospel are largely a sermon on the significance of Jesus as the Christ, written to interpret the religious depth of Christian faith by those who knew their own lives to be made new, it is not surprising that this emphasis is given to the doctrine. Even though the understanding of the Holy Spirit is far from fully developed, still here is the evidence that the Christian fellowship of the end of the first century understood the fact that men and women were called upon to make continually new decisions, yet they could do so strengthened for the purpose by the awareness that they were not alone in the struggle. "But the Comforter, which is the Holy Ghost, whom the Father will send in my name, he shall teach you all things, and bring all things to your remembrance, whatsoever I have said unto you."

The reason that the Holy Spirit is accorded so much recognition is that men and women know in their hearts that though they may sometimes want to retain some moment of exaltation forever, life is not so made that this is possible. Human life has its ups and down, its light and shadow. For many of our insights, this transition from up to down, or from light to shadow, tends to take away the significance. What seemed very important when we were excited and in the presence of an enthusiastic group seems quite dull and tame the next morning. What seemed self-evident in the first flash of insight often becomes obscure and pointless with the passage of time. But when men and women who appreciate the significance and functional use of the symbols of the cross and resurrection use them to live by, they find that this new basis of living can continue to be vital despite changing situations. Indeed, new meaning and deeper value can be found in it as the fellowship experience grows. In the Gospel of John, this essential elasticity of the Christian faith is described in these words: "I have yet many things to say unto you, but ye cannot bear them now. Howbeit when he, the Spirit of truth, is come, he will guide you into all truth: for he shall not speak of himself; but whatsoever he shall hear that shall he speak: and he will show you things to come. He shall glorify me: for he shall receive of mine, and shall show it unto you."

The Christian faith claims to be the new order, because it gives men a new relationship to God which makes possible meaningful living for them. It is a new order that takes seriously the real problems of the real world, and neither denies them nor evades them, but changes men's relationship to them because it first of all rests upon their own changed relationship to life's unconditioned and essential demand. In Christian thinking this new relationship to God is called the doctrine of the holy Trinity. Without it there is no new order of the ages, because without it men have not really come to terms with the underlying religious problems they must face. Without it life remains threatening and confusing. With it there are still problems of history to be dealt with — we do not have world peace, and we do not see poverty eliminated, and we do have problems of conflict between individuals and groups. But men who have interpreted the meaning of their own lives in terms of the cross and resurrection are enabled to live creatively amid real problems. As someone has said, " The Christian gospel does not so much solve problems as it enables us to live with unsolved problems."

The author of the Epistle to the Hebrews understood the way the new order works for living men in this real world. " Thou hast put all things in subjection under his feet. For in that he put all in subjection under him, he left nothing that is not put under him. But now we see not yet all things put under him. But we see Jesus, who was made a little lower than the angels for the suffering of death, crowned with glory and honor; that he by the grace of God should taste death for every man."

CHAPTER XI

The Confident Fellowship

THE most powerful result of living by Christianity is to know oneself to be a member of a confident fellowship. The final test is not in any form of mathematical certainty, but in a group life in which the whole is more than the sum of its parts. Through the life of the Christian group, the spirit of God strengthens the individual members where they need it — in the areas of mutual acceptance, forgiving and asking forgiveness, and love.

Christianity makes sense. It produces a confident fellowship which enables the members to live in a real world without evading or distorting the facts. Within the fellowship we can deal adequately with the problems of death and guilt, because through our association with others, who share our common faith, we are given the courage to trust God's love, even though life may be often difficult, and even though we ourselves may be the most difficult part of life.

Fellowship is primarily a Christian word. The primary Christian sacraments — Baptism and Holy Communion — imply that our spiritual strength is sustained by group life. In Baptism a baby is made a part of this fellowship, so that his growing and unfolding life will be sustained by it as the strongest influence he will know. In Holy Communion, the symbol of the family dinner table, with Jesus Christ himself at the head of the table, becomes the way we see our relationship to him, and to one another and to the world outside.

Our association with one another is on a number of different levels, and perhaps by placing them in a series the meaning of the confident fellowship may be made clearer. There are a lot of people in the concourse of Grand Central Station, New York City, between four thirty and six P.M., every day. They have a common purpose — catching a train to go home. But there is really no bond between them as they run and dodge, and push by each other and bump into each other. On a little higher level of association is the audience at a motion picture, because they are not only in the same building for the same purpose, but they also react to humor or sadness at the same time — but the bond of shared emotion is not really very great.

A baseball stadium finds an even higher level of association, because tradition allows the spectators at ball parks to talk to each other whether or not they are acquainted. Now we have a common purpose, common emotions, and also some interaction. On an even higher level is the association of men in an organization — that of an office, a factory, or perhaps the armed services — because there is associated effort in which each person has to depend on the co-operation of others for the common enterprise to succeed.

A family is perhaps the best illustration of the highest level of human association on natural terms. If there is any fellowship in the world where acceptance becomes a reality, where forgiveness is a possibility, and where people can be valued for being part of the family regardless of other factors, here it is. If a family has any stability, we dare to admit our problems, and to ask help in facing our defeats. We even can dare sometimes to admit our disloyalties to the family itself.

The confident fellowship of Christian faith is the family principle, purified by contact with Jesus Christ, applied to everyday affairs of life. Elton Trueblood has pointed up one aspect of this fellowship in his recent book *Your Other Vocation,* where he suggests that the distinctive mark of a Christian is that he carries his Christianity with him into all kinds of normal relationships — and that this, indeed, is what gives purpose to his life. The other side of the same truth is that we can bring back into the family circle our achievements and failures, our resources and our needs, and find the spiritual support that life demands.

The fifth century liturgical custom known as " Ordo Romanus Primus " illustrates the point. The details are from a much simpler economy, when most people supported themselves by agricultural labor, and when there was little cash money in the average pocket. When families came to Holy Communion, they brought from home a small flask of homemade wine such as they drank themselves, and a small loaf of bread they had baked for their own tables. This was the offertory. From it, bread and wine were taken for the Holy Communion itself; some went for the support of the clergy, who lived the same way their people did, and the rest was given to the poor. People brought to church the very things they used to sustain their own lives — the fruit of their own labor. They received it back symbolically as one or two of the loaves were broken and shared in the congregation and one or two of the flasks of wine were poured into the chalice and passed from communicant to communicant. They then returned to the world to go on with the tasks of Christian living.

Ordo Romanus Primus represents a way of dramatizing dynamically how the Christian fellowship finds its confidence, and how its members are strengthened for daily life through their association in the family life of the Church of Christ. In our more complex economy it is harder to dramatize the same thing and have it become so obviously clear. Many of us work with intangibles — we hand papers back and forth representing in some instances commodities, and in other instances more indirect relationships, and in still other instances an even less direct connection with the economic order. It is not easy to see how insurance policies, bills of lading, stocks and bonds, blueprints, and directions for machine operation can be offered on the altar and then broken and shared. But the principle is still true, even though our imaginations are stretched to appreciate it.

It is in the life of the confident fellowship that Christianity meets the final test of adequacy as the faith that makes sense. The test of any religion takes several forms. It takes, of course, the form of the more severe tests arising from the internal physiological and psychological drives of its make-up. It includes the strains and stresses exerted upon men's faith by changing historical circumstances, particularly when these changes involve wars and depressions which upset normal patterns of living. We have also seen that the test of adequacy involves facing ultimately the question of whether one's understanding of life is functional, not only for oneself but for all men everywhere under all conditions. The issue of universality is not only ethical. It is also a way of asking us whether or not we are deceiving ourselves.

The test of a vital, functioning religion takes one more very practical form. Every religious statement, whether that of a formal tradition or of an implied faith, has to meet the test of contradiction in life. Regardless of what that religion does to deal with the problems of death and guilt in theory, its adequacy is measured by the fact that it can be lived only by men and women who know all too well the contrast between their ideals and their fulfillment. Individuals and groups in this real world reflect and demonstrate only imperfectly and partially the best of theories. The contrast between the ideal, as understood intellectually and, indeed, as experienced religiously on occasions, and the continuing pattern of normal life is sufficiently sharp to make men and women question the value of their religious insights.

The discussion of the meaning of the Trinity was concluded with the passage from the Epistle to the Hebrews: "But now we see not yet all things put under him. But we see Jesus." We do not live in a world that shows many evidences of being organized on the basis of Christian faith. When any honest man looks at the recesses of his own heart — his own undisclosed secrets, fears, ambitions, and desires — or when he looks at the confusion and perplexity of society around him, he sees a world waiting for and needing redemption. He does not see much evidence that it is already redeemed. Even if he appreciates the meaning for his own life of the cross and resurrection, he sees his own inadequacy of performance in the ordinary routines of his daily existence. Indeed, he is probably more conscious than ever of that inadequacy.

The contrast between the world as it ought to be and the world as it is found to be is not peculiar to the Christian insight. The motivating force behind both Pharisee and Sadducee types of religions was an awareness of this contrast, and that something ought to be done about it. It is not sufficient to have an answer that solves life's problems in some ideal manner. The answer must be tested against the actuality of the clash between the ideal and the real in this practical sense. It is obvious that only a general realization of world brotherhood can provide the spiritual basis for world peace, for one example, and it is also obvious that even those who recognize this fact find difficulty in living it consistently in their own private lives and in their group and national activity.

The distinctive thing about the Christian faith is its acceptance of this test as significant. The Sadducee attempts to solve this last problem by reducing his ideal as far as possible to the level of history, and thus eliminates the contrast by selling out. Since he serves as his own god in a functional sense, the significance of the test is destroyed. The Pharisee recognizes the contrast, but he believes that men by consistent moral effort can overcome it. The Sadducee expects no Kingdom of God, except in the terms of getting along himself. The Pharisee has a strong sense of a Kingdom of God in judgment upon, and in contrast to, the world, but he believes that it can be realized in human society here and now if only men work hard enough at the task of getting it. The Christian realizes that the contrast is of the nature of reality itself. He accepts it and lives in it, without selling out to history, on the one hand, and without denying the nature of history on the other.

The Christian faith meets this final test of adequacy for daily living through the doctrine of the holy Catholic Church. This is the symbol that makes the fellowship of those who define the meaning of their lives by the cross and resurrection of Jesus Christ the confident fellowship. Its confidence is based upon its awareness that it can live in this real world, accepting the contradiction between the ultimate solution of life's problems and the historical situation as we meet it, yet still assured that life makes sense regardless, because it knows itself to be composed of forgiven sinners.

The holy Catholic Church is the symbol applied to men that parallels the symbol of the holy Trinity applied to God. It is the description of what men and women can believe and do within history to live the faith, which alone enables them to deal adequately with the problems of death and guilt and to attain a meaningful security, status, and achievement pattern for themselves. Like the symbol of the Trinity, it depends upon a prior encounter with Jesus as the Christ, Jesus as the transforming power, before it has any vital meaning. The holy Catholic Church is not a description of an organization, but of a fellowship which understands its existence in a double relationship — toward God and toward history. It has no reality apart from the living contacts of men with each other, and such contacts involve machinery to handle problems of group life, but it is certainly not contained within any ecclesiastical machinery no matter how old or how honored.

As against the picture given in Dostoevsky's *The Grand Inquisitor* of the institution deliberately sterilizing man's spiritual outreach in order to make life easier for all concerned, the holy Catholic Church, in the Christian sense, is that fellowship which transcends all institutional limitations and the shortsightedness of individuals to encourage men to delve ever more deeply into life's fundamental questions. It is the symbol, therefore, of the fellowship of men created by a common faith and itself directed by the content of that faith. Where institutional life and the gospel are in conflict, the institution is plainly in error, usually because it is the natural tendency of all human institutions to literalize symbols and transform insight into formulas.

Recently, a group of high school juniors were asked whether it was possible to live by the Ten Commandments. One girl in the group replied, "I don't know that it is, but I could do a great deal better at it if I were with others who were also trying to do the same thing." This is, of course, an oversimplification, but it points to something very basic. While there remains an unbridgeable gulf between the facts of history and man's ideal of a perfect world where the victory is won, and while Christian faith has always referred the consummation of man's struggle beyond history, there is, nevertheless, a bridge of the spirit which enables you and me, with our limitations and failures and partial conversion, to be ourselves and to have fellowship with others on that basis.

Dr. H. Richard Niebuhr, of Yale, has developed the symbol the "trialectic" to indicate that the encounter of a faith never takes place in a vacuum. When man responds to life's demand he always does so in a living context, which both colors his understanding of the demand itself and also frames and supports his response. The Christian faith involves a three-way relationship — God and man, God and the fellowship, man and the fellowship. Without the triple character, the whole relationship tends to become abstract or mechanical.

The third paragraph of the Apostles' Creed — " I believe in the Holy Ghost; the holy Catholic Church; the communion of saints; the forgiveness of sins; the resurrection of the body; and the life everlasting " — is a way of stating that man's response by means of the cross and resurrection involves association with others in full fellowship — a fellowship of people standing shoulder to shoulder as they face life's practical transitions and decisions. Man makes his response by means of the cross and resurrection only in the context of the holy Catholic Church. It is through his awareness of fellowship that man knows the power of the Holy Spirit, since it is within the fellowship life that people discover the continuing relevance of the Christian decision.

It is through his awareness of fellowship on the basis of a common faith in the cross and resurrection that man knows both " the forgiveness of sins " and " the resurrection of the body." The Creed plainly states that within the fellowship, created by the response of faith and kept alive and relevant by the Holy Spirit, men are able to deal adequately with both guilt and death. Within this fellowship men need not fear the pressures of their past mistakes and the cumulative error of the world, nor need they fear the unknowable and unforeseeable decisions which lie ahead. Consequently, this fellowship is, for those who take it seriously as the framework of their lives, a " community of all holy people, all holy things," since with death and guilt under control men are able to regard themselves, to regard one another, and to value this created world, as representing the purpose of the Eternal.

But these statements can easily become abstract unless their practical significance is clarified. Paul told the Colossians: "If ye then be risen with Christ, seek those things which are above, where Christ sitteth on the right hand of God. Set your affection on things above, not on things on the earth. For ye are dead, and your life is hid with Christ in God. When Christ, who is our life, shall appear, then shall ye also appear with him in glory. Mortify therefore your members which are upon the earth. . . . Lie not one to another, seeing that ye have put off the old man with his deeds; and have put on the new man, which is renewed in knowledge after the image of him that created him: where there is neither Greek or Jew, circumcision nor uncircumcision, Barbarian, Scythian, bond nor free; but Christ is all, and in all."

This is a statement that where a living fellowship between men is created by their common loyalty to Jesus as their Christ, they are enabled to deal adequately with life's religious problems. This common faith will be reflected in the way they understand one another. After listing various obvious moral implications, Paul declared that for those who frame the meaning of their lives by the fellowship of the cross and resurrection, there can be no ultimate distinctions between people. It is not that men ought to respect one another across the natural lines of division which cut the human race into conflicting segments; it is that in this common faith they do respect one another, because they live now by a different nature — "in knowledge after the image of him that created him." The result of this fellowship is to believe that the unity of the spirit is more significant than the divisions of history. While the latter cannot be ignored, and the tensions between groups have to be dealt with, those who understand the meaning of their own lives in terms of the cross and resurrection have a new relationship to the problems of race and economic class and social background, community and nation and world, which allows them to deal with these problems without defensiveness and without fearing the loss of security, status, and achievement.

In the Epistle to the Galatians, Paul said: "For ye are all the children of God by faith in Christ Jesus. For as many of you as have been baptized into Christ have put on Christ. There is neither Jew nor Greek, there is neither bond nor free, there is neither male nor female: for ye are all one in Christ Jesus."

The divisions between men are of two categories, but both categories continually remind us of the contradiction between the vision of our faith and the pressures of history. One of these categories is evolutionary and the other is of the ultimate structure of life. Human nature is so constructed that functional breakdowns are necessary to get the work of the world done. While some of these breakdowns change with the changes of processes, and others, like male and female, are as old as history and designed to be as long as history, nevertheless, both categories tend to be exploited by man's fear and defensiveness. The social divisions of the communities in which we live are among the most natural defenses against life's questions, but they also signify that the threats of death and guilt are raised in social situations.

In his Letter to the Galatians, Paul pointed out that within the fellowship of faith the functional breakdowns of society were bridged, and a harmony of the spirit achieved. But these breakdowns are not canceled. Male and female are divisions which cannot be ignored — and they have biological, psychological and sociological ramifications. Although the conventions by which society channels relations between the sexes have evolved and changed through human history, the ultimate difference remains, and the difference is of the very stuff of history and cannot be ignored without ignoring history. There are other divisions of the same type, and likewise subject to evolutionary changes in convention and custom, but still of the very structure of human life. Another such division is that between the generations. Children and adults cannot meet on the same plane, even though the details of parent-child relationships have been revised many times in human history and there is still room for improvement. Another such division is that of the languages, for although languages themselves evolve and borrow from each other, all living languages are bearers of culture, of common experience, of a community life, and dreams like that of Esperanto miss the point.

In his Letter to the Galatians, Paul declared that while many of the divisions between men are of the very structure of history and cannot be ignored except at the price of foolishness, nevertheless, they can be transcended by a common faith, in terms of which people may speak to one another across the gulfs that separate them, and thus find a community of purpose and a possibility of fruitful relationship. The effect of the fellowship of faith upon its members is not to deny their differences in social situations, but to transform the differences from occasions for hostility, growing out of the fear of death and guilt, into occasions for brotherhood growing out of the common acceptance of Jesus as the Christ.

Paul in his Letter to the Philippians used another image to describe the fellowship: "We are a colony of heaven" (Moffatt). A colony of retired Roman soldiers lived in a number of provincial towns like that of Philippi, and its members took part in the community life and problems of the towns in which they lived. But they had a paramount loyalty to Rome itself, which they had served in the army and from whence they drew their pensions, and, consequently, they served to bring the Roman spirit continually into the practical issues of the provincial towns. The fellowship of the Christian faith lives in history where practical problems affect everyone. These problems — of home and business and community, of politics, economics, and social life — cannot be ignored by Christians, because they live in a real world. Just as the Roman colonists at Philippi were necessarily concerned with the local water supply as well as with their loyalty to Rome, so the Christian fellowship is necessarily concerned with the real problems of the real world. But there is a difference in the way the colonists and the indigenous inhabitants are related to their problems. The Christian fellowship does not deny the reality of the immediate issues and is concerned about practical problems of administration, but these problems are seen in perspective. Life's meaning does not rise or fall with the outcome of practical projects, important as they may be, but through full participation in the affairs of each day, living a faith that transcends the immediate, releases tension, and frees men for creative action.

The Old Testament view of Israel was of the people of God, the sacred congregation, chosen to work out God's plan in history. The Passover tradition in Judaism is a reminder that Israel was redeemed for a purpose — the fulfillment of the law — by which not only the members of the congregation themselves but the whole wide world might find its true peace and its real meaning. Those who rewrote the history of Israel after the return from Babylon used the traditions and legends to advance this point of view. The doctrine of the remnant, developed during the same period and refined during the four hundred years between the return and the time of Christ, applied this purpose to whatever part of Israel kept the faith and lived up to the covenant. In other words, the Israel of the Old Testament was regarded as a much more literal parallel, so to speak, to the Roman colony, an image which leaves out the missionary dynamic of the Christian fellowship. The Old Testament theory, including that of the remnant, is given a profound pictorial description in the account in Genesis of Abraham interceding with God for the people of Sodom and Gomorrah — " Peradventure there be fifty righteous within the city: wilt thou also destroy and not spare the place for the fifty righteous that are therein? " " Peradventure ten shall be found there? "

The Christian understanding of the role of the fellowship picks up where the Old Testament conception stops. The understanding of being chosen to fulfill God's purposes for all mankind remains, but the manner of choosing and the range of the purpose has been transformed. The doctrine of the remnant — the faithful minority fulfilling God's commandment — is retained and changed. Instead of being a plea for at least a small group to make a success out of the Pharisee approach to life, the remnant is now reduced to one man, who fulfills the law by dying on the cross, but thereby enables all those who are associated with him to acquire a new relationship to life's demands. The doctrine of the holy people continues, but is understood in a new way. It is no longer a question of those who are sons of Abraham by blood and who are related to the covenant by ritual. It is now a question of those who are related to Jesus as the Christ by faith, and the spiritual symbol of holy Baptism supplants the external symbol of circumcision. John the Baptist had preached, " Think not to say within yourselves, We have Abraham to our father: for I say unto you, that God is able of these stones to raise up children unto Abraham." The Christian understanding of the holy Catholic Church is of a fellowship created by God among those men who give the response of faith to the cross and resurrection, and who are thus prepared to live by faith as forgiven people.

The function of the Church is to be the frame of reference for this vital, adequate religion. The role of the Church within history is to be that confident fellowship in which and through which men and women dare to face their real problems creatively — both the perplexities of their private lives and the issues of society. Though history remains unredeemed, since new problems arise and new men are born to face them, nevertheless, the fellowship of the Church goes on reaffirming in every situation its confidence that men may live adequately and realistically here and now by faith in Christ Jesus.